CONTENTS

THE MACAT LIBRARY

The Macat Library is a series of unique academic explorations of seminal works in the humanities and social sciences – books and papers that have had a significant and widely recognised impact on their disciplines. It has been created to serve as much more than just a summary of what lies between the covers of a great book. It illuminates and explores the influences on, ideas of, and impact of that book. Our goal is to offer a learning resource that encourages critical thinking and fosters a better, deeper understanding of important ideas.

Each publication is divided into three Sections: Influences, Ideas, and Impact. Each Section has four Modules. These explore every important facet of the work, and the responses to it.

This Section-Module structure makes a Macat Library book easy to use, but it has another important feature. Because each Macat book is written to the same format, it is possible (and encouraged!) to cross-reference multiple Macat books along the same lines of inquiry or research. This allows the reader to open up interesting interdisciplinary pathways.

To further aid your reading, lists of glossary terms and people mentioned are included at the end of this book (these are indicated by an asterisk [*] throughout) – as well as a list of works cited.

Macat has worked with the University of Cambridge to identify the elements of critical thinking and understand the ways in which six different skills combine to enable effective thinking.
Three allow us to fully understand a problem; three more give us the tools to solve it. Together, these six skills make up the **PACIER** model of critical thinking. They are:

ANALYSIS – understanding how an argument is built
EVALUATION – exploring the strengths and weaknesses of an argument
INTERPRETATION – understanding issues of meaning

CREATIVE THINKING – coming up with new ideas and fresh connections
PROBLEM-SOLVING – producing strong solutions
REASONING – creating strong arguments

To find out more, visit **WWW.MACAT.COM.**

CRITICAL THINKING AND *BLOODLANDS*

Primary critical thinking skill: EVALUATION
Secondary critical thinking skill: REASONING

A flagbearer for the increasingly fashionable genre of "transnational history," Timothy Snyder's *Bloodlands* is, first and foremost, a stunning example of the critical thinking skill of evaluation. Snyder's linguistic precocity allows him to cite evidence in 10 languages, putting fresh twists on the familiar story of World War II fighting on the Eastern Front from 1941-45. In doing so, he works to humanize the estimated 14 million people who lost their lives as their lands were fought over repeatedly by the Nazis and their Soviet opponents.

Snyder also works to link more closely the atrocities committed by Hitler and Stalin, which he insists are far too often viewed in isolation. He focuses heavily on the adequacy and relevance of his evidence, but he also uses the materials he has culled from so many different archives as fuel for an exemplary work of reasoning, forcing readers to confront the grim realities that lie behind terms such as 'cannibalism' and 'liquidation.' In consequence, *Bloodlands* has emerged, only a few years after its publication, as one of the seminal works of its era, one that is key to Holocaust studies, genocide studies and area studies, and to sociology as well as to history. A masterly work of literature as well as of history, *Bloodlands* will continue to be read for decades.

ABOUT THE AUTHOR OF THE ORIGINAL WORK

US historian **Timothy Snyder** is recognized as one of the world's leading experts on Eastern European history.

Born in 1969 in Dayton, Ohio, Snyder wrote his doctoral thesis at Oxford University in England, learning a number of Eastern and Central European languages at the same time. Snyder's writing career soon took off, and it was *Bloodlands: Europe Between Hitler and Stalin* (2010) that really sealed his reputation as an historian. Currently a professor at Yale University, Snyder is often called on to air his views as a political pundit. His views remain controversial – with some accusing him of anti-Russian bias – but he works with various institutions that foster international understanding, such as the International Commission for the Evaluation of the Crimes of the Nazi and Soviet Regimes in Lithuania.

ABOUT THE AUTHOR OF THE ANALYSIS

Dr Helen Roche teaches history at the University of Cambridge, where her work focuses on education and the uses of classicism in Nazi Germany. Her second monograph, *The Third Reich's Elite Schools: A History of the Napolas*, is forthcoming from the Oxford University Press.

ABOUT MACAT

GREAT WORKS FOR CRITICAL THINKING

Macat is focused on making the ideas of the world's great thinkers accessible and comprehensible to everybody, everywhere, in ways that promote the development of enhanced critical thinking skills.

It works with leading academics from the world's top universities to produce new analyses that focus on the ideas and the impact of the most influential works ever written across a wide variety of academic disciplines. Each of the works that sit at the heart of its growing library is an enduring example of great thinking. But by setting them in context – and looking at the influences that shaped their authors, as well as the responses they provoked – Macat encourages readers to look at these classics and game-changers with fresh eyes. Readers learn to think, engage and challenge their ideas, rather than simply accepting them.

'Macat offers an amazing first-of-its-kind tool for
interdisciplinary learning and research. Its focus on works
that transformed their disciplines and its rigorous approach,
drawing on the world's leading experts and educational institutions,
opens up a world-class education to anyone.'

**Andreas Schleicher,
Director for Education and Skills, Organisation for Economic
Co-operation and Development**

'Macat is taking on some of the major challenges in university
education ... They have drawn together a strong team of active
academics who are producing teaching materials that are
novel in the breadth of their approach.'

**Prof Lord Broers,
former Vice-Chancellor of the University of Cambridge**

'The Macat vision is exceptionally exciting. It focuses
upon new modes of learning which analyse and explain seminal texts
which have profoundly influenced world thinking and so social and
economic development. It promotes the kind of critical thinking
which is essential for any society and economy.
This is the learning of the future.'

Rt Hon Charles Clarke, former UK Secretary of State for Education

'The Macat analyses provide immediate access to the critical
conversation surrounding the books that have shaped their
respective discipline, which will make them an invaluable resource
to all of those, students and teachers, working in the field.'

Professor William Tronzo, University of California at San Diego

WAYS IN TO THE TEXT

KEY POINTS

- Timothy Snyder, one of the world's leading experts on Eastern European history, is currently a professor at Yale University.*

- His book *Bloodlands* argues that we need to treat all the mass killing that occurred in Eastern Europe between 1933 and 1945 in one single narrative that takes account of all the victims.

- The work's insights can help us to understand the global tragedy of World War II* (1939–45) and the Holocaust* —the mass-murder of at least six million European Jews* committed in the years of the war.

Who Is Timothy Snyder

Timothy Snyder, the author of *Bloodlands: Europe Between Hitler and Stalin* (2010), was born in 1969 in Dayton, Ohio.* He studied at Brown University* and Oxford University,* where he wrote his doctoral thesis. During his time at Oxford, Snyder was able to learn several Eastern and Central European languages that would prove crucial for his research.[1]

After he gained his doctorate, Snyder soon began to make his name as a historian of Eastern Europe. He wrote a series of biographies and a book on Central European nationalism* (a belief in the superiority of one's own country over others). Many of these were well reviewed, and some won prizes. In 2001, he was appointed Bird White Housum Professor of History at Yale University.[2] But it was *Bloodlands: Europe between Hitler and Stalin* that really made his name.

Since *Bloodlands* appeared, Snyder has become a political pundit as well as a scholar. He often comments on current affairs in the media, especially the *New York Review of Books*, in connection with Eastern Europe.[3] He is also involved with various institutions that foster international understanding, such as the International Commission for the Evaluation of the Crimes of the Nazi* and Soviet* Regimes in Lithuania,* a commission appointed by the president of Lithuania.[4] "Nazi" here refers to the extreme right-wing German Nazi Party, led by the dictator Adolf Hitler* through the years of World War II; "Soviet" refers to the Soviet Union, a federation of communist states in Eastern Europe and Central Asia that existed from 1922 until 1991, led from the Russian capital, Moscow.

Snyder's political views have sometimes been considered controversial. Certain critics have accused his historical analysis of revealing a pro-Polish, pro-Ukrainian, and anti-Russian bias.[5] Others see *Bloodlands* as equating the crimes of Hitler's Germany and Joseph Stalin's* Soviet Union[6] (Stalin was the leader of the Soviet Union in the years 1922–53). Snyder's latest book, *Black Earth: The Holocaust as History and Warning* (2015), has also sparked much debate.[7] For the time being, then, his career as a global superstar historian looks set to continue.

What Does *Bloodlands* Say?

Bloodlands argues that previous histories have kept Nazi and Soviet crimes unduly separate, focusing more on the Holocaust than on Stalin's crimes against humanity. They have emphasized Western Europe over Eastern Europe. They immortalize Auschwitz,* the Polish site of a million murders in the latter years of World War II, but not the killing fields of the East, where many millions were starved or executed on account of agricultural policy and political repression. Snyder claims that we need a history of World War II that depicts all victims' suffering. This includes the Holocaust—but it also includes the sufferings of Ukrainians in the famines that Stalin caused, and the sufferings of Poles and the Baltic peoples under both Hitler and Stalin.

The title of the book is a coinage, invented by Snyder himself. He defines the "bloodlands" as including Poland, the Baltic states* (Estonia, Latvia, and Lithuania), Ukraine, and the eastern edge of Soviet Russia. In the bloodlands, he states, 14 million people—not soldiers, but civilians—died during World War II.

Snyder argues that the peoples in the bloodlands suffered most because they were caught between the Soviet and Nazi regimes. They had to undergo not a single invasion, nor even a double invasion. Instead, they were subjected to three invasions, first by the Soviets, then by the Nazis, and then again by the Soviets. Each invasion brought more brutality and slaughter than the last. The two regimes reacted against each other in an escalating cycle of violence.

Snyder's book synthesizes a vast amount of scholarship. He has used archival documents and secondary literature in 10 different languages, bringing new sources and new interpretations to public attention for the very first time. In this way, *Bloodlands* has begun fundamentally to reframe the ways we think about World War II and the Holocaust. It has not only inspired academic debate—though there has been much of this—it has also been used by Eastern European nations to foster new forms of identity politics. For instance, translations of the book in the Eastern European nations of Ukraine and Georgia* have been freely distributed to counter pro-Stalinist* Russian narratives.[8]

Bloodlands's enduring importance can be shown by the fact that the book was translated into more than 30 languages between 2010 and 2014.[9] It has also been published in multiple editions, and won numerous prizes, including the Hannah Arendt Prize, a German prize awarded by an international jury, and the Leipzig Prize for European Understanding. The book's arguments continue to shape historical debates about World War II and the Holocaust, as well as Eastern European memory politics in the present day. Finally, the term "bloodlands" has swiftly become a standard term in discussions of this period.

Why Does *Bloodlands* Matter?

Bloodlands is a groundbreaking work of transnational* history (that is, it analyzes the history shared by several nations). It encourages us to think outside traditional national frameworks, and to make new connections. It asks the reader to lay aside preconditioned assumptions—about the uniqueness of the Shoah* (another name for the Holocaust) or the relative barbarity of Nazism and the aggressively dictatorial version of the social and economic system of communism* practiced in the Soviet Union.

Above all, *Bloodlands* appeals to our humanity. Snyder shows us why history is a "humanities" discipline in the most meaningful sense. He is careful to portray the countless dead as individual people who lived, rather than meaningless strings of statistics. In order to understand how people can commit atrocities, he argues, we need to lay moral judgment to one side. But we must still have compassion for the victims.

Bloodlands also helps us to combat assumptions about the relative importance of Western Europe. Just because the "bloodlands" may be less familiar does not make them less significant. Such insights can help to foster a more enquiring mind-set. They encourage readers to leave their comfort zone.

This is also true of some of the brutalities that Snyder describes. By making readers confront the true horror of cannibalism or mass shooting, he forces them to reflect on what humanity is capable of. His descriptions might even spur us on to take action against present-day atrocities or genocides* (mass killings of a specific group of people).

Bloodlands stands at the intersection of many disciplines. Although Snyder does not engage in much theoretical discussion, his insights are useful for sociologists* as well as historians. The book has also become a key text in Holocaust studies, genocide studies, and area studies* (inquiry into the culture, history, and geography of a particular region), as well as in history. Snyder even presents some more philosophical reflections in his introduction and conclusion. Moreover, the book's prose is so well crafted that it deserves to be treated as a work of literature as well as a work of history. Any reader will find new ideas to take away from *Bloodlands*—whether a turn of phrase, a metaphysical question, or a historical concept.

Finally, the book helps to explain how one of the greatest disasters in history—the slaughter unleashed by World War II and the Holocaust—could have come to pass. Between them, Hitler and Stalin brought about a tragedy that shook the whole world. That tragedy still shapes politics and current affairs today. *Bloodlands* helps us come closer to understanding both its genesis, and its global effects.

NOTES

1   Zbigniew Truchlewski, "Timothy Snyder, A Historian of Eastern Europe," *Nouvelle Europe [en ligne]*, February 11, 2013, accessed February 25, 2016, http://www.nouvelle-europe.eu/node/1640.

2   Yale University Department of History website, "Timothy Snyder," accessed February 25, 2016, http://history.yale.edu/people/timothy-snyder.

3   Examples include: Timothy Snyder, "A Fascist Hero in Democratic Kiev," The *New York Review of Books*, February 24, 2010; Timothy Snyder, "Ukrainian Extremists Will Only Triumph if Russia Invades," *New Republic*, April 17, 2014, accessed February 25, 2016, https://newrepublic.com/article/117395/historic-ukrainian-russian-relations-impact-maidan-revolution; Timothy Snyder, "The Battle in Ukraine Means Everything: Fascism Returns to the Continent It Once Destroyed," *New Republic*, May 11, 2014, accessed February 25, 2016, https://newrepublic.com/article/117692/fascism-returns-ukraine; Timothy Snyder, "Edge of Europe, End of Europe," The *New York Review of Books*, July 21, 2015, accessed February 25, 2016, http://www.nybooks.com/blogs/nyrblog/2015/jul/21/ukraine-kharkiv-edge-of-europe/.

4   "Timothy Snyder," http://history.yale.edu/people/timothy-snyder.

5   See, for example, Dovid Katz, "Detonation of the Holocaust in 1941: A Tale of Two Books," *East European Jewish Affairs* 41, no. 3 (2011): 207–21.

6   See, for example, Daniel Lazare, "Timothy Snyder's Lies," *Jacobin*, September 9, 2014.

7   See, for example, Walter Laqueur, "Timothy Snyder: The Newton of the Holocaust?" *Mosaic*, November 4, 2015, accessed February 25, 2016, http://mosaicmagazine.com/observation/2015/11/timothy-snyder-the-newton-of-the-holocaust/.

8   Artur Komilienko, "Snyder's 'Bloodlands' Released in Russian Despite Deadlock to Publish in Russia," *Kyiv Post*, July 13, 2015, accessed February 25, 2016, www.kyivpost.com/content/ukraine/snyders-bloodlands-released-in-russian-despite-deadlock-to-publish-in-russia-393339.html; Heinrich Böll Foundation South Caucasus, "Rethinking Stalinist History Through the Publication of Timothy Snyder's *Bloodlands: Europe Between Hitler and Stalin* (2014)," September 27, 2014, accessed February 25, 2016, https://ge.boell.org/en/2014/09/27/rethinking-stalinist-history-through-publication-timothy-snyders-bloodlands-europe.

9   Michael Pinto-Duschinsky, "Hitler's 'Ecological Panic' Didn't Cause the Holocaust," *Standpoint*, September 2015, accessed February 25, 2016, http://www.standpointmag.co.uk/node/6189/full.

SECTION 1
INFLUENCES

MODULE 1
THE AUTHOR AND THE HISTORICAL CONTEXT

KEY POINTS

- *Bloodlands* is the first popular history to consider the crimes committed by the Nazi* leader Adolf Hitler* and the Soviet* leader Joseph Stalin* in Eastern Europe during 1933–45 in a single narrative, stressing the brutal interaction between their regimes on local populations.

- While Snyder originally intended to use his doctorate in Eastern European history to open the door to a diplomatic career, once he had determined to become a historian, he was swiftly able to make a name for himself in his chosen field.

- The fall of the Iron Curtain*—the militarized border between Europe's communist* nations and the democratic nations to the west—played an important part in turning Snyder's focus toward Eastern Europe during his doctoral studies.

Why Read this Text?

Timothy Snyder's *Bloodlands: Europe Between Hitler and Stalin* (2010) is the first major popular history of World War II* and the Holocaust* to focus on the killing fields of Eastern Europe. Unlike many previous works, it considers atrocities committed by Adolf Hitler and Joseph Stalin in a single overarching narrative, emphasizing connections between the actions of the Nazi and Soviet regimes. In particular, Snyder argues that what he calls the "bloodlands" (Poland, the Baltic states* [Estonia, Latvia, and Lithuania], Ukraine, and the edge of Soviet Russia) suffered from the murderous interaction between the two

> ❝ We have stories about why we do things ... one of the relevant things is generational. The first Solidarity* of 1980–81 was perhaps the event in Europe which forced me to think about the people behind the Iron Curtain as human beings ... The first Solidarity forced people to make distinctions between Poland and Russia, between Poland's government and Poland's people. And that was extremely important, not because I understood it, I was eleven years old at that time, but because it forced me to think about that world as a world with a complicated history, where there are people. ❞
>
> Timothy Snyder, in Zbigniew Truchlewski, "Timothy Snyder, A Historian of Eastern Europe," *Nouvelle Europe*

regimes, undergoing the brutalities of a threefold invasion.

Bloodlands is a key example of the turn toward transnational* history—that is, looking beyond history-writing centered on single nations, and trying to find connections and contacts between different countries. It has also become highly influential in Holocaust studies; indeed, some scholars even see the work as heralding a new wave of scholarship that does not insist upon the uniqueness of the Holocaust, but allows for fruitful comparison with other genocides.*[1] Even Snyder's coinage of the word "bloodlands" has swiftly been taken up by other scholars working on this period, as well as by the media.

Bloodlands has been extraordinarily successful; a worldwide best seller, it has already gone into multiple editions, and been translated into more than 30 languages. The book has been awarded numerous "Book of the Year" titles, and has also won several prizes, including the Hannah Arendt Prize and the Leipzig Prize for European Understanding.[2]

Author's Life

Born in 1969 in a small town in the US state of Ohio,* Timothy Snyder began his academic career with a degree in political science, economics, and philosophy at Brown University,* only switching to study history toward the end of his undergraduate course.³ He then succeeded in gaining a coveted Marshall scholarship to write a doctoral thesis on the life of the Polish philosopher and sociologist Kazimierz Kelles-Krauz* at the University of Oxford,* jointly supervised by the historians Timothy Garton Ash* and Jerzy Jedlicki.*⁴

At first, Snyder—whose family had lived in southwestern Ohio for two centuries and who had no Jewish or Eastern European ancestry— thought that he would simply use the Polish, Czech, Ukrainian, and other languages that he had learned during his doctorate as the springboard for a career in the foreign service. As he told one interviewer, "I grew up as an American kid with no connection to any of these places … I thought I was going to grow up and become a diplomat and negotiate nuclear arms."⁵ However, he soon came to love "the archival work, the travel, and the sense of discovery" involved in historical research so much that he wholeheartedly accepted Garton Ash's suggestion that he should make his career as a historian instead.⁶

During the course of the 2000s, Snyder began to make his name as a historian of Eastern Europe with a series of critically and popularly acclaimed works, including two further biographies (of the Polish artist and politician Henryk Józewski* and the aristocratic Ukrainian statesman Wilhelm von Habsburg* respectively), and a study of nation-building in Poland, Lithuania, Ukraine, and Belorussia.⁷ In 2001, he also gained a professorship at Yale University in the United States. However, it was the publication of *Bloodlands* in 2010 that launched Snyder into the highest echelons of academic celebrity. Since the book's publication, he has been much in demand as a political commentator and pundit, writing regularly for periodicals such as the *New York Review of Books, New Republic,* and the *Times Literary Supplement.* It seems likely that his latest book, *Black Earth: The Holocaust as History and Warning,* will continue to secure his status as a renowned, if somewhat controversial, figure in Eastern European history and politics.[8]

Author's Background

Snyder attributes a great deal of importance to the fact that he was just beginning to come of age as a scholar at exactly the point that the Iron Curtain fell: "It was precisely the revolutions of 1989 and the beginning of change in Eastern Europe which drew my attention away from Russia and Germany and towards Eastern Europe."[9] For the first time, it seemed that the long period of tension between the United States and the Soviet Union known as the Cold War,* and the rule of the Soviet Union over the nations of Eastern Europe known as the Eastern bloc,* would not last forever—and the idea of studying Eastern Europe held a new excitement and promise.

Moreover, there was now an enormous amount of new material to be discovered in the archives that had formerly been under Soviet control. Recollecting his feelings at the time, Snyder muses, "Partly it was an excitement about those revolutions ... there was this idea that people who had thoughts were now going to have power. That's a very simple, naïve way of putting it, but it was fascinating for me at that time, and ... I'm still interested in ... this tradition of the intelligentsia and the idea of people who have a role in national culture, thinking about national politics. This is the tradition that mattered then, and it matters now."[10]

Snyder has also stressed the importance of his studies at Oxford for defining his choice of career path. First, it was easy for him both to spend the requisite amount of time learning multiple Eastern European languages, and to make frequent journeys to Europe for archival research. Second, the university had just instigated a series of exchanges with Czech, Polish, and other Eastern and Central European students, known as the Soros fellowships, which gave Snyder an unprecedented entry into their national cultures. This, in turn, confirmed him in his conclusion that Eastern Europe was "a part of the world where many of the most important events of world history actually played out."[11]

NOTES

1   See further Daniel Blatman, "Holocaust Scholarship: Towards a Post-Uniqueness Era," *Journal of Genocide Research* 17, no. 1 (2015), 21–43.

2   For a full list, see Snyder's CV, available at Yale University Department of History website, "Timothy Snyder," accessed February 25, 2016, http://history.yale.edu/people/timothy-snyder.

3   Zbigniew Truchlewski, "Timothy Snyder, A Historian of Eastern Europe," *Nouvelle Europe [en ligne]*, February 11, 2013, accessed February 25, 2016, http://www.nouvelle-europe.eu/node/1640.

4   Timothy Snyder, *Nationalism, Marxism, and Modern Central Europe: A Biography of Kazimierz Kelles-Krauz (1872–1905)* (Cambridge, MA: Harvard University Press, 1998), xiii–xiv.

5   David Mikics, "The Diplomat of Shoah History: Does Yale Historian Timothy Snyder Absolve Eastern Europe of Special Complicity in the Holocaust?" *Tablet*, July 26, 2012, accessed February 25, 2016, http://www.tabletmag.com/jewish-arts-and-culture/books/107382/diplomat-of-shoah-history.

6   *Connecticut Jewish Ledger* eds., "Q & A with … Prof. Timothy Snyder: Best-selling Author of *Bloodlands: Europe Between Hitler and Stalin*," *Connecticut Jewish Ledger*, September 22, 2011, accessed February 25, 2016, http://www.jewishledger.com/2011/09/q-a-with-prof-timothy-snyder-best-selling-author-of-bloodlands-europe-between-hitler-and-stalin/.

7   Timothy Snyder, *Sketches from a Secret War: A Polish Artist's Mission to Liberate Soviet Ukraine* (New Haven: Yale University Press, 2005); Timothy Snyder, *The Red Prince: The Fall of a Dynasty and the Rise of Modern Europe* (London: Bodley Head, 2008); Timothy Snyder, *The Reconstruction of Nations: Poland, Ukraine, Lithuania, Belarus, 1569–1999* (New Haven: Yale University Press, 2003).

8   Walter Laqueur, "Timothy Snyder: The Newton of the Holocaust?" *Mosaic*, November 4, 2015, accessed February 25, 2016, http://mosaicmagazine. com/observation/2015/11/timothy-snyder-the-newton-of-the-holocaust/.

9   Truchlewski, "Timothy Snyder."

10   Truchlewski, "Timothy Snyder."

11   Truchlewski, "Timothy Snyder."

MODULE 2
ACADEMIC CONTEXT

KEY POINTS

- *Bloodlands* can be seen as a new milestone in the debate over the comparability of Nazi* and Soviet* atrocities that had polarized opinion during the "Historians' Dispute"* of the late 1980s.

- Given its focus on victimhood in Eastern Europe, *Bloodlands* also represents a significant contribution to the field of Holocaust* studies.

- Snyder's most prominent intellectual influences include the British historians Timothy Garton Ash,* Tony Judt,* and Norman Davies.*

The Work In Its Context

The scholarly terrain that Timothy Snyder set out to rechart in *Bloodlands: Europe Between Hitler and Stalin*—namely, the genesis of the Holocaust, and Nazi and Soviet atrocities during World War II*—has long been a highly contested area. For decades, historians of twentieth-century Europe, particularly in Germany, had been constantly alert to the pitfalls of comparing the crimes of Hitler* and Stalin* within the framework of totalitarianism theory*—a theory arguing for equivalence between extreme right fascist* and extreme left communist* dictatorships, focusing on similarities in ideology, the presence of a one-party state, a state terror apparatus, a state monopoly on violence and mass communication, and centralized decision-making. As Jörg Baberowski* has noted, "Nobody could write about the excesses of Stalinist violence without acknowledging that the Nazi murder program was unique. Nonetheless everybody knew, even then, that uniqueness cannot be established without comparisons and contrasts."[1]

> ❝ The new multinational histories of the Shoah are a very recent phenomenon. For decades, most Holocaust historians focused solely on the Nazi perpetrators. The first wave of Holocaust history, under [Raul] Hilberg's influence, insisted on seeing the event through German eyes, and Hilberg disagreed sharply with younger historians' interest in the life stories of Hitler's Jewish victims … He advocated, instead, a wide-angle perspective on how the vast work of killing occurred. ❞
>
> David Mikics, "The Diplomat of Shoah History: Does Yale Historian Timothy Snyder Absolve Eastern Europe of Special Complicity in the Holocaust?" *Tablet*

In the late 1980s, the discipline reached a crisis point in the form of the so-called Historians' Dispute (*Historikerstreit*), in which several conservative German historians were castigated for their apparent equation of Nazi and Soviet brutalities.[2] The historian Ernst Nolte,* foremost among their number, was particularly vilified for publishing an opinion piece in the *Frankfurter Allgemeine Zeitung* newspaper that suggested that Nazi crimes might actually have been inspired by prior "Asiatic" atrocities committed by the Soviets.[3] In this context, even a couple of decades ago, it would have been tantamount to scholarly suicide for Snyder to publish a book that focused so extensively on treating the barbarities of the Hitler and Stalin regimes side by side—even though, as the author himself stresses, the argument "that the Soviets were just as bad as the Germans is … a polemical and indefensible view."[4]

From another perspective, Snyder's work represents a flowering of the resurgent interest in Central and Eastern European history that has followed the raising of the Iron Curtain* (the border between the democratic Western state and the communist Eastern states of Europe) in 1991.[5] Following in the tradition of scholars such as Norman

Davies, whose work put Poland on the map in terms of popular history, *Bloodlands* refocuses our attention on those countries that were caught between Nazi Germany and the Soviet Union, and whose history has often been marginalized in mainstream accounts of World War II.[6]

Overview of the Field

Bloodlands has also been hailed as making a significant—and potentially groundbreaking—contribution to the constantly expanding field of Holocaust studies. While the earliest histories, such as the Austrian Raul Hilberg's* study of the destruction of European Jewry,* focused almost exclusively on the perspective of the perpetrators of the Holocaust,[7] more recent works, particularly the Israeli historian Saul Friedländer's* monumental Holocaust history, have concentrated on incorporating the perspective of the victims themselves.[8] Arguably, Snyder's emphasis in *Bloodlands* on the fate of the victims of Nazi and Soviet atrocities whom he insistently describes as individuals—whether they be Jewish, Polish, Ukrainian, or any other nationality or ethnicity—owes something to Friedländer's approach.[9]

Within Holocaust studies, Snyder's turning away from matters connected with the extermination centers of Central Europe (what he has called the "concentration camp* universe") and toward the killing fields of Eastern Europe also has its antecedents in books such as the US historian Christopher Browning's* *Ordinary Men: Reserve Police Battalion 101 and the Final Solution in Poland* (1992), and the US author Daniel Jonah Goldhagen's* best selling, if controversial, *Hitler's Willing Executioners: Ordinary Germans and the Holocaust* (1996).[10] Both of these works focused on the activities of German police battalions who were involved in the mass shooting of Jews in the newly conquered Eastern territories of the Third Reich*—as Germany under the Nazis called itself.

More recently, however, historians such as the Israeli-born Omer

Bartov* have also pleaded for an end to the "hegemony of Third Reich history over the field of Holocaust history," seeking to foster a renewal of interest in the "perspectives, languages, actions and reactions of the Jewish and even non-Jewish victims of the Nazi terror in those areas where the Holocaust actually happened: east of Germany."[11] In a sense, *Bloodlands* could be interpreted as Snyder's response to precisely this plea.

Academic Influences

Some critics have taken Snyder to task—both in connection with *Bloodlands*, and with some of his other works—for his resolute refusal to engage in meaningful historiographical* debate (debate on approaches to the writing of history texts), or to frame his research in terms of his predecessors' scholarly achievements.[12] Nevertheless, it is still possible to determine some of his intellectual influences, starting with those figures who were his mentors while he was still a student.

Within the pages of *Bloodlands* itself, Snyder acknowledges his debt to Mary Gluck,* professor of history and Judaic studies at Brown University,* his *alma mater*, and to Timothy Garton Ash, his doctoral supervisor at Oxford.* He also mentions the significance of his conversations with Tony Judt, a leading historian of Europe with whom he had collaborated in writing an intellectual history of the twentieth century, based on interviews conducted during the final stages of Judt's terminal illness.[13] Snyder also praises a number of his colleagues for their impact upon his thought, including the Berlin-based historian Ray Brandon* and Piotr Wandycz,* his predecessor at Yale University,* and remarking that "a decade of agreeing and disagreeing with Omer Bartov, [the Polish-born historian] Jan Gross,* and [the US historian] Norman Naimark* in various settings has sharpened my thinking on a host of questions."[14] Finally, he credits the British historian Norman Davies with drawing his attention, in an article published in the *New York Review of Books*, to "some of the shortcomings of previous approaches" to the problems treated in *Bloodlands*.[15]

NOTES

1   Jörg Baberowski, "Once and For All: The Encounter Between Stalinism and Nazism. Critical Remarks on Timothy Snyder's *Bloodlands*," *Contemporary European History* 21, no. 2 (2012): 145.

2   For more on this, see Charles Maier, *The Unmasterable Past: History, Holocaust, and German National Identity* (Cambridge, MA: Harvard University Press, 1988); Richard J. Evans, *In Hitler's Shadow: West German Historians and the Attempt to Escape from the Nazi Past* (New York: Pantheon, 1989).

3   Ernst Nolte, "Vergangenheit, die nicht vergehen will: Eine Rede, die geschrieben, aber nicht mehr gehalten werden konnte," *Frankfurter Allgemeine Zeitung*, June 6, 1986.

4   Sönke Neitzel, "Im Kerngebiet des Todes," *Frankfurter Allgemeine Zeitung*, January 29, 2012; quotation from David Mikics, "The Diplomat of Shoah History: Does Yale Historian Timothy Snyder Absolve Eastern Europe of Special Complicity in the Holocaust?" *Tablet*, July 26, 2012, accessed February 25, 2016, http://www.tabletmag.com/jewish-arts-and-culture/books/107382/diplomat-of-shoah-history.

5   On Slavic studies as an emerging field in this context, see Mark von Hagen, "Empires, Borderlands and Diasporas: Eurasia as Anti-Paradigm for the Post-Soviet Era," *American Historical Review* 109, no. 2 (2004): 445–68, especially 445.

6   David Herman, "Why Bloodlands is Still One of the Books of the Year," *New Statesman*, October 3, 2010, accessed February 25, 2016, http://www.newstatesman.com/blogs/cultural-capital/2010/12/soviet-snyder-history-europe.

7   Raul Hilberg, *The Destruction of the European Jews* (New Haven: Yale University Press, 1961).

8   Saul Friedländer, *Nazi Germany and the Jews: The Years of Persecution, 1933–1939* (New York: Harper Collins, 1997); Saul Friedländer, *The Years of Extermination: Nazi Germany and the Jews, 1939–1945* (New York: Harper Collins, 2007).

9   For more on this, see Thomas Kühne, "Great Men and Large Numbers: Undertheorizing a History of Mass Killing," *Contemporary European History* 21, no. 2 (2012): 136.

10 Christopher Browning, *Ordinary Men: Reserve Police Battalion 101 and the Final Solution in Poland* (New York: Harper Collins, 1992); Daniel Jonah Goldhagen, *Hitler's Willing Executioners: Ordinary Germans and the Holocaust* (New York: Knopf, 1996).

11 Kühne, "Great Men and Large Numbers," 134; Omer Bartov, "Eastern Europe as the Site of Genocide," *Journal of Modern History* 80, no. 3 (2008), 557–93.

12 Kühne, "Great Men and Large Numbers," 136–7; Michael Pinto-Duschinsky, "Hitler's 'Ecological Panic' Didn't Cause the Holocaust," *Standpoint*, September 2015, accessed February 25, 2016, http://www.standpointmag. co.uk/node/6189/full.

13 Timothy Snyder, *Bloodlands: Europe between Hitler and Stalin* (London: Vintage, 2015), 420; Tony Judt with Timothy Snyder, *Thinking the Twentieth Century* (London: Heinemann, 2012).

14 Snyder, *Bloodlands*, 420.

15 Snyder, *Bloodlands*, 421; see further Norman Davies, "The Misunderstood Victory in Europe," The *New York Review of Books*, May 25, 1995, accessed February 25, 2016, http://www.nybooks.com/articles/1995/05/25/the-misunderstood-victory-in-europe/.

MODULE 3
THE PROBLEM

KEY POINTS

- *Bloodlands* aims to redirect perspectives on the Holocaust* toward Eastern Europe, taking a transnational* standpoint (an attempt to analyze the role of several nations in a larger historical narrative).

- In *Bloodlands*, Timothy Snyder was able to unite a variety of viewpoints on World War II* that had previously often been separated: those of Holocaust scholars, and those of historians of the Soviet* and Nazi* regimes.

- Snyder has criticized scholars such as the Polish-born historian Jan Gross* for taking what he deems an overly microhistorical* approach to the Holocaust (an approach focusing on very specific details); in *Bloodlands*, he prefers to focus on the bigger questions.

Core Question

Timothy Snyder's *Bloodlands: Europe Between Hitler and Stalin* can be considered in the context of works contributing to the debate about the genesis of the Holocaust, and the question of how supposedly civilized European nations could so quickly have descended into such lethal brutality and genocide* during the mid-twentieth century. Until quite recently, histories of World War II tended to focus either upon the military conflict itself, or on the Holocaust, or they tended to focus upon the experience of one nation state.[1] However, sparked by what has been termed the "transnational turn," a new wave of historians—including Timothy Snyder in *Bloodlands*, and the British historian Mark Mazower* in *Dark Continent: Europe's Twentieth Century* and *Hitler's Empire: Nazi Rule in Occupied Europe*—have

> ❝ To become a historian of Eastern Europe is to become aware of the Holocaust, and of other German crimes, in a different way. The Holocaust happened entirely behind the line that became the Iron Curtain.* And the opening of the Iron Curtain, the possibility of living and researching in Eastern Europe, was a special opportunity for my generation. As I worked on other East European subjects, I came to feel that East Europeanists had a responsibility to write about the Holocaust. ❞
>
> Timothy Snyder, Interview with the *Connecticut Jewish Ledger*

attempted to find a paradigm (roughly, an analytical framework) for the history of World War II that can "rescue History from the Nation"[2]; that is, look beyond an analysis of the historical contribution made by any specific nation.

While many scholars in Holocaust studies have recently tended to focus on the micro level, exploring individual communities where Jews* were murdered in exhaustive detail, and relying heavily on survivor testimony, Snyder sees this as "dodg[ing] the biggest question: why the Holocaust took place in Eastern Europe rather than elsewhere."[3] In an interview with *Tablet* magazine, Snyder has stated that "actually figuring out how Soviet power mattered, how it made possible the murder of Jews as well as all the other murders, is the true theme of *Bloodlands*."[4]

By focusing on the murderous *interaction* between the Nazi and Soviet regimes, which primarily took place in the territories of Eastern Europe, *Bloodlands* aims to highlight an important element in the genesis of the Holocaust that Snyder felt had been previously overlooked.[5]

The Participants

As the American historian Christopher Browning* recently noted in a roundtable critique of *Bloodlands*, Snyder uses the Eastern European geographical context of his study to "unite three histories which he says have been kept separate: the Holocaust, Hitler's* other victims, and the mass killings of Stalin."*[6] Scholarship dealing with violence and atrocity in Eastern Europe has tended to be divided along two lines. Authors are primarily interested in either a) linking the Holocaust with wider Nazi programs of ethnic cleansing* (ridding a territory of a certain ethnic group) and demographic revolution, or b) in comparative genocide (whether the comparison is being made with other victims of the Nazi regime, such as the handicapped, or with other genocidal regimes.)[7] "Demographic" here refers to the statistical makeup of a population.

Leading lights in Holocaust studies such as Christopher Browning, the German historians Peter Longerich* and Michael Wildt,* and the French historian Christian Ingrao,* have tended toward the former path, often focusing on the actions of Nazi perpetrators, and siting the Holocaust squarely within the context of German history.[8] Meanwhile, depictions of atrocities under Stalin have also tended to sit broadly within a Russian historiographical* framework—the British American historian Robert Conquest's* *Harvest of Sorrow* and the American historian Norman Naimark's* *Stalin's Genocides* perhaps being cases in point.[9] Snyder's originality therefore lay in the skillful way in which he was able to weave together these disparate strands, linking "Stalin's mass killings ... and the intensifying interaction between the two dictators" more compellingly than anyone before him had been able or willing to do.[10]

The Contemporary Debate

In *Bloodlands*, Snyder sees himself very much as providing grand, large-scale explanations, as opposed to dabbling in microhistory* (conducting research in which a specific event or person is studied). In this vein, he has sometimes gone so far as to set himself up in opposition to scholars such as the Israeli scholar Omer Bartov* and the Polish–born historian Jan Gross, at times even criticizing them outright for failing to grasp the bigger picture: "So, Omer [Bartov] writes a book about the [German] army [during World War II], then he writes a book about [his ancestral home town in the Ukraine,] Buczacz,"* Snyder noted in an interview with David Mikics. "The concern is that when you get that intimate and that small, you can't really catch the big things. You see that in [Jan Gross' book] *Neighbors* … it can't really have full explanations."[11]

In more general terms, Snyder has acknowledged his debt to the work of mainstream Holocaust scholars, including Peter Longerich, Saul Friedländer,* and Christopher Browning. Indeed, he admits that his interpretation of the escalation of the "Final Solution,"* Nazi Germany's policy of exterminating Jewish people, and the precise point at which "the prior Nazi determination to rid Europe of Jews became concrete policy during the war and … as a consequence of the war," owes much to his interpretation of their contributions to Holocaust historiography.[12]

NOTES

1 See David Mikics, "The Diplomat of Shoah History: Does Yale Historian Timothy Snyder Absolve Eastern Europe of Special Complicity in the Holocaust?" *Tablet*, July 26, 2012, accessed February 25, 2016, http://www.tabletmag.com/jewish-arts-and-culture/books/107382/diplomat-of-shoah-history.

2 Mark Mazower, *Dark Continent: Europe's Twentieth Century* (London: Penguin, 1999); Mark Mazower, *Hitler's Empire: Nazi Rule in Occupied Europe* (London: Penguin, 2008). See further Tara Zahra, "Imagined Noncommunities: National Indifference as a Category of Analysis," *Slavic Review* 69, no. 1 (2010): 93–119, 94.

3   Mikics, "The Diplomat of Shoah History."

4   Mikics, "The Diplomat of Shoah History."

5   See for example Timothy Snyder, *Bloodlands: Europe between Hitler and Stalin* (London: Vintage, 2015), vii–xi, xix.

6   Christopher Browning, "H-Diplo Roundtable Review of Timothy Snyder, *Bloodlands: Europe between Hitler and Stalin*," *H-Diplo Roundtable Reviews* 13, no. 2 (2011), 9.

7   Examples of these two approaches include Henry Friedlander, *The Origins of Nazi Genocide: From Euthanasia to the Final Solution* (Chapel Hill: University of North Carolina Press, 1995); Robert Melson, *Revolution and Genocide: The Origins of the Armenian Genocide and the Holocaust* (Chicago: University of Chicago Press, 1992).

8   See for example Christopher Browning, *The Origins of the Final Solution: The Evolution of Nazi Jewish Policy, September 1939–March 1942* (Lincoln: University of Nebraska Press, 2004); Peter Longerich, *Holocaust: The Nazi Persecution and Murder of the Jews* (Oxford: Oxford University Press, 2010); Christian Ingrao, *Believe and Destroy: Intellectuals in the SS War Machine* (Cambridge: Polity Press, 2013); Michael Wildt, *An Uncompromising Generation: The Nazi Leadership of the Reich Security Main Office* (Madison: University of Wisconsin Press, 2010).

9   Robert Conquest, *The Harvest of Sorrow: Soviet Collectivization and the Terror-Famine* (Oxford: Oxford University Press, 1986); Norman Naimark, *Stalin's Genocides* (Princeton: Princeton University Press, 2010). See also Ray Brandon and Wendy Lower, eds., *The Shoah in Ukraine: History, Testimony, Memorialization* (Bloomington: Indiana University Press, 2008).

10   Browning, "Roundtable Review," 9.

11   Mikics, "The Diplomat of Shoah History." Snyder is referring here to Omer Bartov, *The Eastern Front, 1941–1945: German Troops and the Barbarization of Warfare* (Basingstoke: Palgrave Macmillan, 2001), and Jan Gross, *Neighbors: The Destruction of the Jewish Community in Jedwabne, Poland* (Princeton: Princeton University Press, 2001).

12   *Encyclopedia Britannica* eds., "The Stalinist and Nazi Killing Machines: 5 Questions for Bloodlands Author Timothy Snyder," *Encyclopedia Britannica Blog*, March 14, 2011.

MODULE 4
THE AUTHOR'S CONTRIBUTION

KEY POINTS

- In *Bloodlands*, Timothy Snyder seeks to redirect attention from the horrors of the Nazi* concentration camps* toward the killing fields of Eastern Europe, where many millions of other people lost lives to famine, warfare, and execution.

- Snyder's coinage of the term "bloodlands" for the areas in which local populations suffered at the hands of both the Nazi and Soviet* regimes has added an important new dimension to twentieth-century European history.

- Snyder was partly inspired to focus on the Eastern European victims of Hitler* and Stalin* by the British Polish historian Norman Davies,* and in particular by his essay "The Misunderstood Victory in Europe" (1995).

Author's Aims

"For the time being," Timothy Snyder concludes in the coda to *Bloodlands: Europe Between Hitler and Stalin,* "Europe's epoch of mass killing is overtheorized and misunderstood."[1] In avoiding the seductions of using academic theories—whether those concerned with totalitarianism* (the state's intrusive intervention in the life of the citizen), modernity, genocide,* or whatever else—to try to explain the slaughter that occurred in Eastern Europe during World War II,* Snyder is able to focus instead on providing a clear, if horrific, narrative of what happened to the victims of both the Nazi and Soviet regimes.

In so doing, Snyder's aims are broadly twofold. First, he wishes to refocus attention on the killing fields of Eastern Europe, and the barbarities that all of the peoples there suffered at the hands of Hitler and Stalin—and not just the Jews.*[2] He wants to situate the

> **66** Killing people turns them into numbers. For instance, at this massacre at Sandy Hook, [a] school ... about 25 miles from here, I can tell you that there were 26 school children who were killed. I cannot tell you all their names and what they were like. But the murder created the number 26. Just like the Holocaust created six million. The killers create the numbers, but then what we remember are the numbers. And the numbers are not neutral. In some sense they are the creation of other individuals and those numbers have a power, which continues long after the deed. **99**
>
> Timothy Snyder, in Zbigniew Truchlewski, "Timothy Snyder, A Historian of Eastern Europe," *Nouvelle Europe*

Holocaust* within the context of the 14 million noncombatant casualties that took place in what he calls the "bloodlands," an area he defines as including "Poland, the Baltic States,* Soviet Belarus, Soviet Ukraine, and the western fringe of Soviet Russia"—the area of the greatest civilian slaughter.[3]

Moreover, Snyder sees the Western European imagination as dangerously fixated on the Nazi death camps as the site of the Holocaust at the expense of all else. In his view, however, "the image of the German concentration camps as the worst element of [Nazism] is an illusion, a dark mirage over an unknown desert ... Auschwitz* ... was not the height of the technology of death; the most efficient shooting squads killed faster, the starvation sites killed faster ..." Referencing the musical terms "coda" (a closing passage), and "fugue" (a somewhat complicated music form), he concludes by remarking that Auschwitz was merely "the coda to the death fugue."[4]

Approach

The most obviously original aspect of *Bloodlands* was Snyder's coinage of the very idea of the "bloodlands." According to his own definition, "the bloodlands [were the] territories subject to *both* German and Soviet police power and associated mass killing policies at some point between 1933 and 1945 ... This is a history of the people killed by the policies of distant leaders. The victims' homelands lay between Berlin and Moscow; they became the bloodlands after the rise of Hitler and Stalin."[5] Even if other scholars had attempted to find a fresh interpretive framework for considering Central and Eastern Europe— such as the Israeli historian Omer Bartov's* concept of the "shatterzone of empires"—their ideas did not quite possess the same horrific immediacy as Snyder's newly-coined expression.[6]

Another key aspect of Snyder's narration is his desire to reclaim the fates of individuals from the numbing numerical statistics of mass slaughter. Indeed, the fates of a select group of individuals are crucial to the form the book takes in its composition; when we first encounter these people at the moment of death, on the very first page of *Bloodlands*, they are nameless.[7] In the conclusion, however, we return to these vignettes to find the individuals who suffered them christened and humanized: "Each of the living bore a name."[8] In the final paragraphs, Snyder lays out his rationale even more clearly: "Each of the 21,892 Polish prisoners of war shot by the [Soviet secret police] in 1940 was in the midst of life. The two at the end might be Dobiesław Jakubowicz, the father who dreamed about his daughter, and Adam Solski, the husband who wrote of his wedding ring on the day that the bullet entered his brain."[9] Snyder sees this endeavor as forming a crucial part of the "humanistic" duty of the historian—to give the massed ranks of victims back a little of their humanity.[10]

In more general terms, Snyder's ability to read and interpret a vast amount of primary and secondary material, including literatures in 10 different languages, enabled him to put forward a compelling synthesis of current research on the topic.[11] Arguably, few other scholars would have had the ability or the erudition to match this undertaking.

Contribution in Context

Snyder commonly makes reference to the intellectual debt he owes to the historian Norman Davies, particularly in relation to an article Davies published in the *New York Review of Books* in 1995, entitled "The Misunderstood Victory in Europe."[12] In this essay, Davies asked, "How often do you hear what I think probable, that the largest number of civilian casualties of the war in Europe was sustained by the Ukrainians?"[13] This question, and the inadequacy of responses to it, led Snyder toward a more sustained engagement with the identities of the victims of Stalinism*—the political ideology of the Soviet leader Joseph Stalin—and Nazism, as well as leading him toward the conclusion that "the war, at least as far as civilian casualties were concerned, was an East European war."[14]

Snyder also explicitly draws on arguments put forward by the historians Peter Longerich* and Christian Gerlach,* both noted for their work on the Holocaust, when it comes to explaining the exact point at which the Nazi extermination of the Jews became concrete policy.[15] Indeed, some of Snyder's critics have taken him to task for merely providing a synthesis of "facts and interpretations culled from established authorities: Christian Streit* on the Soviet [prisoners-of-war]; Christian Gerlach on 'hunger politics'; Nicolas Werth* and Lynne Viola* on the Ukrainian famine; Dieter Pohl* and Karel C. Berkhoff* on German-occupied Ukraine; Peter Longerich, Christopher Browning,* and Andrej Angrick* on the Holocaust," rather than presenting new evidence and substantially new arguments.[16]

Meanwhile, in terms of implicit comparison of the dictatorships led by Hitler and Stalin, Snyder also fits into a tradition of writing that considers the two dictators and their rule in parallel, whose leading exponents include the British historians Alan Bullock* and Richard Overy,* and the Canadian historian Robert Gellately.*[17] More stringent critics have taken this likeness further, describing Snyder as a "son" or "grandson" of Ernst Nolte,* the conservative German historian who attempted to excuse Nazi atrocities by casting them as a preemptive defense against Soviet brutalities.[18]

NOTES

1 Timothy Snyder, *Bloodlands: Europe between Hitler and Stalin* (London: Vintage, 2015), 383.

2 Snyder, *Bloodlands*, 384.

3 Snyder, *Bloodlands*, viii–xi.

4 Snyder, *Bloodlands*, 382–3; see also xi–xv. Snyder is referring here to Paul Celan's Holocaust poem *Todesfuge* ("Death Fugue"), first published in 1948.

5 Snyder, *Bloodlands*, 409, xix.

6 See the volume based on his project: Omer Bartov and Eric D. Weitz, eds., *Shatterzone of Empires: Coexistence and Violence in the German, Habsburg, Russian, and Ottoman Borderlands* (Bloomington: Indiana University Press, 2013).

7 Snyder, *Bloodlands*, vii.

8 Snyder, *Bloodlands*, 379.

9 Snyder, *Bloodlands*, 408.

10 Snyder, *Bloodlands*, 408.

11 See for example Snyder, *Bloodlands*, 413–14.

12 John Connelly, "Gentle Revisionism," in "Review Forum: Timothy Snyder, *Bloodlands: Europe between Hitler and Stalin*," by John Connelly et al., *Journal of Genocide Research* 13, no. 3 (2011): 314.

13 Norman Davies, "The Misunderstood Victory in Europe," The *New York Review of Books*, May 25, 1995, accessed February 25, 2016, http://www.nybooks.com/articles/1995/05/25/the-misunderstood-victory-in-europe/.

14 Connelly, "Gentle Revisionism," 314–15; see Snyder, *Bloodlands*, 421.

15 Timothy Snyder, "A New Approach to the Holocaust," The *New York Review of Books*, June 23, 2011, accessed February 25, 2016, http://www.nybooks.com/articles/archives/2011/jun/23/new-approach-holocaust/#fn-7; *Encyclopedia Britannica* eds., "The Stalinist and Nazi Killing Machines: 5 Questions for Bloodlands Author Timothy Snyder," *Encyclopedia Britannica Blog*, March 14, 2011.

16 Omer Bartov, "Review of *Bloodlands: Europe between Hitler and Stalin* by Timothy Snyder," *Slavic Review* 70, no. 2 (2011): 425. The works to which Bartov refers in this quotation include: Christian Streit, *Keine Kameraden: Die Wehrmacht und die sowjetischen Kriegsgefangenen 1941–1945* (Bonn: Dietz, 1991); Christian Gerlach, *Kalkulierte Morde: Die deutsche Wirtschafts—und Vernichtungspolitik in Weißrußland 1941 bis 1944* (Hamburg: Hamburger Edition, 1999); Nicholas Werth, *La terreur et le désarroi: Staline et son système* (Paris: Perrin, 2007); Lynne Viola, *Peasant Rebels Under Stalin: Collectivization and the Culture of Peasant Resistance* (New York: Oxford University Press, 1996); Lynne Viola, *The Unknown Gulag: The Lost World of Stalin's Special Settlements* (New York: Oxford University Press, 2007); Dieter Pohl, *Verfolgung und Massenmord in der NS-Zeit 1933–1945* (Darmstadt: Wissenschaftliche Buchgesellschaft, 2003); Karel Berkhoff, *Harvest of Despair: Life and Death in Ukraine Under Nazi Rule* (Cambridge, MA: Harvard University Press, 2004); Peter Longerich, *Politik der Vernichtung: Eine Gesamtdarstellung der nationalsozialistischen Judenverfolgung* (Munich: Piper, 1998); Peter Longerich, *The Unwritten Order: Hitler's Role in the Final Solution* (Stroud: Tempus, 2001); Christopher Browning, *The Origins of the Final Solution: The Evolution of Nazi Jewish Policy, September 1939–March 1942* (Lincoln: University of Nebraska Press, 2004); Andrej Angrick, *Besatzungspolitik und Massenmord: Die Einsatzgruppe D in der südlichen Sowjetunion 1941–1943* (Hamburg: Hamburger Edition, 2003); Andrej Angrick and Peter Klein, *The "Final Solution" in Riga: Exploitation and Annihilation, 1941–1944* (New York: Berghahn Books, 2009).

17 Alan Bullock, *Hitler and Stalin: Parallel Lives* (London: Fontana, 1998); Richard Overy, *The Dictators: Hitler's Germany, Stalin's Russia* (New York: Norton, 2004); Robert Gellately, *Lenin, Stalin, and Hitler: The Age of Social Catastrophe* (New York: Knopf, 2007). See also the informative edited volumes compiled by Ian Kershaw and Moshe Lewin, and by Michael Geyer and Sheila Fitzpatrick: Ian Kershaw and Moshe Lewin, eds., *Stalinism and Nazism: Dictatorships in Comparison* (Cambridge: Cambridge University Press, 1997); Michael Geyer and Sheila Fitzpatrick, eds., *Beyond Totalitarianism: Stalinism and Nazism Compared* (Cambridge: Cambridge University Press, 2009).

18 For examples, see Daniel Lazare, "Timothy Snyder's Lies," *Jacobin*, September 9, 2014, accessed February 25, 2016. https://www.jacobinmag.com/2014/09/timothy-snyders-lies/; Clemens Heni, "Ernst Nolte's grandson," *Defending History.com*, accessed February 29, 2016, http://defendinghistory.com/ernst-noltes-grandson/39530.

SECTION 2
IDEAS

MODULE 5
MAIN IDEAS

KEY POINTS

- *Bloodlands* considers the atrocities and mass killings carried out by both the Nazi* and Soviet* regimes within a single narrative, rejecting all forms of national or ethnic exceptionalism (that is, without singling out any nation's actions, or the predicament of any specific people, as singularly important).

- In *Bloodlands*, Timothy Snyder stresses the importance of the interactions between the Nazi and Soviet regimes in causing violence and slaughter to escalate.

- In terms of style, *Bloodlands* has frequently been praised for its literary and poetic qualities, as well as for its groundbreaking introduction of new terminology to the scholarly debate.

Key Themes

In essence, Timothy Snyder's *Bloodlands: Europe Between Hitler and Stalin* aims to combat Holocaust* exceptionalism and nationalist narratives of victimhood: "Attention to any single persecuted group, no matter how well executed as history, will fail as an account of what happened in Europe between 1933 and 1945."[1] In Snyder's view, both the Holocaust and national tragedies such as the Holodomor,* the Ukrainian famine of 1932–33 caused by Stalin's agricultural policies, have to be seen in the context of a whole series of episodes of mass killing of civilians that took place in what he calls the "bloodlands" of Eastern Europe: Belarus, the Baltic states, Poland,* and Ukraine.

For Snyder, whether the mass killing was instigated by the Nazi regime or the Soviet regime is, in a sense, immaterial; what matters

" Today there is widespread agreement that the mass killing of the twentieth century is of the greatest moral significance for the twenty-first. How striking, then, that there is no history of the bloodlands. Mass killing separated Jewish history from European history, and East European history from West European history. Murder did not make the nations, but it still conditions their intellectual separation, decades after the end of National Socialism and Stalinism. This study brings the Nazi and Soviet regimes together, and Jewish and European history together, and the national histories together. It describes the victims, and the perpetrators. "

Timothy Snyder, *Bloodlands: Europe Between Hitler and Stalin*

most is that, "during the consolidation of National Socialism* and Stalinism* (1933–1938), the joint German–Soviet occupation of Poland (1939–1941), and then the German–Soviet war (1941–1945), mass violence of a sort never before seen in history was visited upon this region"[2] ("National Socialism" here signifies the extreme right-wing ideology of Nazism). To this end, his narrative runs simply and chronologically through a whole gamut of Nazi and Stalinist atrocities, beginning with the Soviet famines of the mid-1930s, moving through the joint Nazi and Soviet invasion of Poland and the escalation of the Holocaust, and ending with the ethnic cleansings* and renewed Soviet anti-Semitism*—violent hostility to Jewish people—that followed the end of World War II.*

Exploring the Ideas

Put simply, *Bloodlands* argues that "without an account of all of the major killing policies in their common European historical setting, comparisons between Nazi Germany and the Soviet Union must be inadequate. Now that this history ... is complete, the comparison remains."[3] Particularly important in Snyder's reading, however, is the interaction between the Nazi and Soviet dictatorships. Ultimately, he argues, so much blood was spilled in the "bloodlands" only because these territories suffered not single, not double, but triple occupation— first under Stalin,* then under Hitler* after the German invasion of Soviet territory, and finally under Stalin again, as the Soviet military, the Red Army,* pushed ahead to defeat Nazi Germany once and for all. Borrowing a term originally coined by the French historian François Furet,* he characterizes the escalation of violence caused by the two regimes' interactions as a form of "belligerent complicity."[4]

Thus, Snyder portrays the Nazi and Soviet regimes as embarking upon a dance of death whose steps were essentially reactive; for instance, he sees Hitler's "colonial demodernization" of formerly Soviet territories as a response to Stalin's "modernization [of the Soviet Union] by way of self-colonization"[5]— aggressive attempts to change the fabric of a nation as a means of imposing an ideology or as a weapon of war. Meanwhile, although the killing of civilians after Germany invaded the Soviet Union in 1941 did not follow a conventional pattern of reprisals, "in German-occupied Soviet Belarus the Soviets encouraged partisan activity [resistance], and the Germans executed more than three hundred thousand people in return."[6]

Language and Expression

Bloodlands has frequently been praised for the highly literary—or even poetic—quality of its prose. Simply narrated, avoiding high-flown theorizing or academic jargon, Snyder's book is designed to appeal to the widest possible audience: this is popular history in every sense of the word. Take, for instance, the following passage, which captures the intensity and concision of Snyder's writing:

"Fourteen million people were deliberately murdered by two regimes over twelve years. This is a moment that we have scarcely begun to understand, let alone master. By repeating exaggerated numbers, Europeans release into their culture millions of ghosts of people who never lived. Unfortunately, such specters have power. What begins as competitive martyrology can end with martyrological imperialism. The wars for Yugoslavia* in the 1990s began, in part, because Serbs* believed that far larger numbers of their fellows had been killed in the Second World War than was the case. When history is removed, numbers go upward and memories go inward, to all of our peril."[7]

A martyr is someone who loses his or her life for an important cause; "martyrology" is a somewhat ironic term Snyder coins for the almost-religious way that the dead are discussed.

Snyder has also been praised for his "highly effective use of vivid and unflinching descriptions of … actual crimes," and for using individual stories "to open a window onto the past for the reader."[8]

However, *Bloodlands* is also notable for the number of new terms that it brings to the debate on World War II and the Holocaust. The coinage of the term "bloodlands" itself represents a significant contribution, as does Snyder's translation of Furet's term "belligerent complicity." However, Snyder also introduces concepts such as "Molotov–Ribbentrop Europe" for the territories caught between Hitler and Stalin (an allusion to the Molotov–Ribbentrop Pact* of 1939, a treaty of nonaggression signed by the Soviet foreign minister Vyacheslav Molotov and the German foreign minister Joachim von Ribbentrop), "psychic Nazification" (referring to the mind-set of local collaborators with the Nazis), or "de-Enlightenment" (referring to the systematic slaughter of the Polish intelligentsia by both regimes).[9] Finally, Snyder is also extremely careful in the way he uses terminology—as demonstrated by his detailed discussion of his reasons for deliberately avoiding the controversial term "genocide"* in favor of the expression "mass killing."[10]

NOTES

1   Timothy Snyder, *Bloodlands: Europe between Hitler and Stalin* (London: Vintage, 2015), xix.

2   Snyder, *Bloodlands*, viii.

3   Snyder, *Bloodlands*, 381.

4   Snyder, *Bloodlands*, 415.

5   Snyder, *Bloodlands*, 415–16.

6   Snyder, *Bloodlands*, 415.

7   Snyder, *Bloodlands*, 406.

8   Andriy Portnov, "On the Importance of Synthesis and the Productiveness of Comparison," in "Review Forum: Timothy Snyder, *Bloodlands: Europe between Hitler and Stalin*," by John Connelly et al., *Journal of Genocide Research* 13, no. 3 (2011): 328.

9   Snyder, *Bloodlands*, 119, 196, 415.

10 Snyder, *Bloodlands*, 412–13.

MODULE 6
SECONDARY IDEAS

KEY POINTS

- In *Bloodlands*, Timothy Snyder puts forward a novel critique of theories that stress the modernity (the distinctly modern character) of the Holocaust.*

- *Bloodlands* also argues that the escalation of the Holocaust was caused by the desire of the Nazis to snatch some form of victory from the jaws of defeat, as Germany's military destruction began to seem ever more probable.

- In general, Snyder's views on the Holocaust have tended to receive more attention from critics than his interpretations of Soviet* atrocities.

Other Ideas

In *Bloodlands: Europe Between Hitler and Stalin*, Timothy Snyder succeeds in putting forward a number of new interpretations of European history during World War II,* over and above his central thesis, which emphasizes the necessity of treating all the atrocities that took place in Eastern Europe within a single overarching narrative.

First, Snyder goes out of his way to frame *Bloodlands* with a sharp critique of explanations of the Holocaust that treat it as an inevitable product both of the European cultural movement known as the Enlightenment,* with its emphasis on rationality, social reform, and scientific explanation, and of the rise of "modernity."[1] This concern is closely linked with his desire to refocus his readers' attention on the killing fields of Eastern Europe as the most important site of the Shoah,* rather than the concentration camps,* which have often been portrayed as the pinnacle of murderous modernity.[2]

Second, Snyder draws upon a large amount of previous literature

> ❝ In some arguments, German (and Soviet) killing policies are the culmination of modernity, which supposedly began when the Enlightened ideas of reason in politics were practiced during the French Revolution* and the Napoleonic Wars.* The pursuit of modernity in this sense does not explain the catastrophe of 1941 ... Both regimes rejected the optimism of the Enlightenment: that social progress would follow a masterly march of science through the natural world. Hitler and Stalin both accepted a late-nineteenth-century Darwinistic* modification: progress was possible, but only as a result of violent struggle between races or classes. ❞
>
> Timothy Snyder, *Bloodlands: Europe Between Hitler and Stalin*

on the Holocaust in order to put forward the idea that the escalation of the "Final Solution"* (the Nazis' policy of the total extermination of Europe's Jews*) was an attempt by the Final Solution's prime mover, Heinrich Himmler,* on Adolf Hitler's* behalf, to salvage at least one possible form of "victory" in a war that was otherwise quickly becoming unwinnable.[3]

Exploring the Ideas

Some critics have taken strong issue with Snyder's claim that the mass killing that took place in Eastern Europe during World War II is currently "overtheorized and misunderstood,"[4] in particular the German historian Thomas Kühne,* who gave his review of *Bloodlands* the subtitle "Undertheorizing a History of Mass Killing."[5] Nevertheless, Snyder provides a trenchant, if brief, critique of the modernizing view of the Holocaust (which he characterizes as having been put forward by the German American philosopher Hannah

Arendt),* "of people (victims and perpetrators alike) losing their humanity, first in the anonymity of mass society, then in a concentration camp."[6] He argues above all that such theories, which focus on the impact of totalitarian* states on their own citizens, cannot explain the murderous interaction of the two regimes: "Arendt's account of totalitarianism centers on the dehumanization *within* modern mass industrial society, not the historical overlap *between* German and Soviet aspirations and power."[7]

Meanwhile, in the sixth chapter of *Bloodlands*, Snyder explores how the setbacks the German army suffered after invading Soviet Russia impacted on the course of the "Final Solution." Broadly speaking, Snyder argues that Hitler aimed to create four utopias following the invasion—"a lightning victory that would destroy the Soviet Union in weeks; a Hunger Plan that would starve thirty million people in months; a Final Solution that would eliminate European Jews after the war; and a Generalplan Ost* that would make of the western Soviet Union a German colony."[8] Once it became clear that none of these plans would be easily achievable in the near future, Snyder claims that, in the later months of 1941, "Himmler ignored what was impossible, pondered what was most glorious, and did what could be done: kill the Jews east of the Molotov–Ribbentrop line*"— that is, throughout the bloodlands.[9] The situation on the battlefield might not be going to plan, but declaring the conflict to be a "war against the Jews," as Hitler did in 1941, ostensibly meant that some form of victory might nevertheless be salvaged, despite the Wehrmacht's* lack of immediate success in the field (the "Wehrmacht" is the name given to the armed forces of Nazi Germany).[10]

Overlooked

In general terms, more attention has been paid to Snyder's interpretation of the Holocaust than to his examination of Soviet atrocities. Snyder's depiction of the Ukrainian famine of 1932–33 caused by the Soviet leader Joseph Stalin's* agricultural polices, the Holodomor,* and the grievous crimes to which it led—including parents turning to cannibalism and consuming the flesh of their own children, in order to cheat death a little longer—is arguably one of the most harrowing passages in the recent literature on Europe's dark twentieth century.[11] Nevertheless, it is surprising how many reviewers and critics have failed to single this particular episode out—although it goes without saying that there are exceptions to this trend.[12]

Another example of this phenomenon, and one that has been even less discussed during debate on *Bloodlands*, is the argument Snyder implicitly puts forward in the final chapter dealing with the policies and ideology of the Soviet leader Joseph Stalin, Stalinism;* the chapter is headed "Stalinist Antisemitism.*"[13] In Snyder's reading, Stalin can be seen at the very least as having had the potential to finish the Holocaust that Hitler began, had his timely death not intervened. In some form, Stalin's plan for a purge of the Jews, fuelled by a fatal paranoia that he was being murdered at the hands of his Jewish doctors, could be seen as the Soviet answer to the Holocaust. Instead, critics have tended to focus on what they see as Snyder's obfuscation of anti-Semitic Holocaust collaboration* by local populations (the citizens of the Baltic states,* Ukrainians, and Poles).[14]

NOTES

1 Timothy Snyder, *Bloodlands: Europe between Hitler and Stalin* (London: Vintage, 2015), x–xv, 156, 380–7.

2 See in particular Zygmunt Bauman, *Modernity and the Holocaust* (Cambridge: Polity Press, 1989).

3 Snyder, *Bloodlands*, 187–223.

4 Snyder, *Bloodlands*, 383.

5 Thomas Kühne, "Great Men and Large Numbers: Undertheorizing a History of Mass Killing," *Contemporary European History* 21, no. 2: 133–43.

6   Snyder, *Bloodlands*, 380. See further Hannah Arendt, *The Origins of Totalitarianism* (New York: Harcourt, Brace, 1951).

7   Snyder, *Bloodlands*, 381. For more of Snyder's views on the subject, see his interview with Zbigniew Truchlewski: "Timothy Snyder, A Historian of Eastern Europe," *Nouvelle Europe [en ligne]*, February 11, 2013, accessed February 29, 2016, http://www.nouvelle-europe.eu/node/1640.

8   Snyder, *Bloodlands*, 187.

9   Snyder, *Bloodlands*, 189.

10 Snyder, *Bloodlands*, 188.

11 Snyder, *Bloodlands*, 21–58.

12 For example: István Deák, "The Charnel Continent," *New Republic*, December 2, 2010, accessed February 25, 2016, https://newrepublic.com/article/79084/snyder-bloodlands-hitler-stalin; Dan Duray, "Body Count: Timothy Snyder Strips the Holocaust of Theory," *Observer*, February 11, 2010, accessed February 25, 2016, http://observer.com/2010/11/body-count-timothy-snyder-strips-the-holocaust-of-theory/; Adam Muller, "Review of *Bloodlands: Europe between Hitler and Stalin* by Timothy Snyder," *Winnipeg Review*, April 24, 2011, accessed February 25, 2016, http://winnipegreview.com/2011/04/bloodlands-by-timothy-snyder/; Ron Rosenbaum, "Stalin's Cannibals. What the New Book *Bloodlands* Tells Us About the Nature of Evil," *Slate*, February 7, 2011, accessed February 25, 2016, http://www.slate.com/articles/life/the_spectator/2011/02/stalins_cannibals.single.html.

13 Snyder, *Bloodlands*, 339–77.

14 See for example Omer Bartov, "Review of *Bloodlands: Europe between Hitler and Stalin* by Timothy Snyder," *Slavic Review* 70, no. 2 (2011): 424–8; Grzegorz Rossolinski-Liebe, "Review of *Bloodlands: Europa zwischen Hitler and Stalin* by Timothy Snyder," *H-Soz-Kult*, March 30, 2011. Accessed February 25, 2016, http://www.hsozkult.de/publicationreview/id/rezbuecher-15680; Robert Rozett, "Diminishing the Holocaust: Scholarly Fodder for a Discourse of Distortion," *Israel Journal of Foreign Affairs* 6, no. 1 (2012): 60.

MODULE 7
ACHIEVEMENT

KEY POINTS

- *Bloodlands* has arguably achieved its goal of refocusing popular attention on the killing fields of Eastern Europe.

- The reception of *Bloodlands* has benefited from the turn toward transnational* history and area studies* as well as from its broad geographical scope, which has facilitated its translation into many languages.

- Scholars on the left of the political spectrum have tended to criticize *Bloodlands* for its unsympathetic portrayal of the Soviet Union.*

Assessing The Argument

If glowing reviews are anything to go by, then the intentions that Timothy Snyder set out to realize in *Bloodlands: Europe Between Hitler and Stalin* have been fully achieved.[1] The term "bloodlands" itself has swiftly become a key term in scholarship on this area and period, and many of Snyder's central arguments and terms have subsequently made their way into both academic and public debate on the topics at hand.[2]

Meanwhile, Snyder's refocusing of the popular imagination of the Holocaust* and its attendant atrocities toward the mass killing sites at the heart of Eastern Europe has been so successful that he has at times been accused of a bias in favor of the nations concerned. The Israeli scholar Dan Diner* has noted *Bloodlands's* "distinctive, albeit moderate [focus on Poland, leading] at some points … to some slight factual readjustments."[3] More forcibly, the historian Omar Bartov* has claimed that "the book is … permeated by a consistent pro–Polish bias and fails to critically engage with Polish policies and attitudes."[4]

> ❝ Snyder is perhaps the most talented younger historian of modern Europe working today. Astonishingly prolific, he grounds his work in authoritative mastery of the facts, mining tomes of information in multiple languages and brilliantly synthesizing his findings … *Bloodlands* is valuable for its astounding narrative integration of a gruesome era of European history. The upshot of this perspective is that Snyder generally avoids high-flown theoretical propositions in order to give individuals their due, even if just to record their agony and demise. A preternaturally gifted prose stylist, he strives for a moral urgency appropriate to his depressing topics … ❞
>
> Samuel Moyn, "Between Hitler and Stalin," *The Nation*

In sum, if the substance of Snyder's main arguments may occasionally be abhorred, they cannot be ignored. Although no book can claim to have the last word on its subject, the US historian John Connelly's* summation of the achievement of *Bloodlands* seems apt in this context: "One might compare Snyder's role as pioneer in the study of the bloodlands to that of a geographer who explores and describes exotic landforms. Some day geologists, scientists purporting to explain how those landforms emerged, may follow in his path."[5] With *Bloodlands*, Snyder has arguably provided a well-grounded and inspiring foundation for future scholars in his chosen field.

Achievement in Context

In writing *Bloodlands*, Snyder has been able to benefit from a number of recent trends in academia. Not only is it no longer a capital offence to write a book that treats the Nazi* and Soviet regimes together, but "transnationalism"—writing histories that cross national borders, and involve significant elements of comparison between countries—has become one of the most fashionable movements in contemporary history writing. For the past decade and more, historians worldwide have been subscribing to views similar to those Snyder put forward: "When you want to understand a national history, you have to break out of the national framework in order to do [so]."[6] Moreover, *Bloodlands* has also benefited from the rise of the subdiscipline of area studies, particularly in relation to Eastern Europe since the fall of the Iron Curtain*—and Snyder has also become a leading exponent of this form of study.[7]

However, the most impressive weapon in Snyder's scholarly arsenal has always been his command of a vast array of Romance, Slavic, and Germanic languages (Romance languages are languages descended from Latin, and include French and Italian). In an interview with *Tablet* magazine, Snyder made it clear that he believes that this linguistic expertise constitutes one of his best qualifications for writing about this period of Eastern European history: "There's a basic problem with the history of the Holocaust ... The people who do it don't know the necessary languages ... [the German historian Saul Friedländer's]* books, and in general the big books we know about the Holocaust, are basically books about Germany."[8]

Finally, the fact that Snyder's work does cover such a broad geographical spectrum, in some cases contributing to the creation of nationalist narratives of victimhood in the former Eastern bloc,* has ensured its translation into a plethora of languages, as well as (in some cases) gaining the book a cult following, particularly in the Ukraine.*[9] "A nationalist narrative of victimhood" is an account of history in which the suffering of a nation's people is held to be unique and is used to support a specific political agenda.

Limitations

At first glance, the limitations of *Bloodlands* are not wholly obvious.

Numerous reviewers have portrayed the book as representing the highest caliber of transnational, multifaceted, interdisciplinary history—history drawing on the methods and specialist knowledge of different academic disciplines. In a similar vein, Snyder himself has been hailed as making important, if not groundbreaking, contributions to the history of the Holocaust, of Eastern Europe, of World War II,* and of the twentieth century in general.[10] The debate stirred up by the book's original publication is still going strong, and seems set to continue into the future, as Snyder provides more fodder for controversy with his more recent forays into the history of this period.[11]

Nevertheless, *Bloodlands* has received its fair share of criticism, if not downright vilification, particularly from scholars further to the left of the political spectrum.[12] As one reviewer pointed out in the British journal *The Economist*, "*Bloodlands* has aroused fierce criticism from those who believe that the Soviet Union, for all its flaws, cannot be compared to the Third Reich,* which pioneered ethnic genocide.*"[13]

This hostility perhaps attained its most colorful manifestation in a book-length rebuttal published by Grover Furr,* a medieval literary scholar turned trenchant supporter of Russian head of state Vladimir Putin.* Furr's book was entitled *Blood Lies: The Evidence That Every Accusation Against Joseph Stalin* and the Soviet Union in Timothy Snyder's Bloodlands Is False.*[14] Other critics have raised concerns that, wittingly or unwittingly, Snyder's argument "legitimises ultranationalists in eastern Europe who downplay the Holocaust, exaggerate their own suffering—and dodge guilt for their own collaboration with Hitler's* executioners."[15]

NOTES

1   Examples include: Zina Gimpelvich, "Review of *Bloodlands: Europe between Hitler and Stalin* by Timothy Snyder," *Canadian Slavonic Papers/Revue Canadienne des Slavistes* 53, no. 2/4 (2011): 634–36; David Herman, "Review of *Bloodlands: Europe between Hitler and Stalin* by Timothy Snyder," *New Statesman*, November 30, 2010, accessed February 25, 2016, http://www.newstatesman.com/books/2010/11/million-soviet-snyder-europe; Justin McCauley, "Book Review: Timothy Snyder's *Bloodlands*," The *Vienna Review*, May 20, 2012, accessed February 25, 2016, http://www.viennareview.net/vienna-review-book-reviews/book-reviews/it-tolls-for-thee; Ian Thomson, "Review of *Bloodlands: Europe between Hitler and Stalin* by Timothy Snyder," The *Telegraph*, November 9, 2010, accessed February 25, 2016, http://www.telegraph.co.uk/culture/books/bookreviews/8120244/Bloodlands-Europe-Between-Hitler-and-Stalin-review.html.

2   See for example Jacek Kurczewski, ed. *Reconciliation in Bloodlands: Assessing Actions and Outcomes in Contemporary Central-Eastern Europe* (Oxford: Peter Lang, 2014); Norman W. Spaulding, "Resistance, Countermemory, Justice," *Critical Enquiry* 41, no. 1 (2014): 144.

3   Dan Diner, "Topography of Interpretation: Reviewing Timothy Snyder's *Bloodlands*," *Contemporary European History* 21, no. 2 (2012): 127.

4   Omer Bartov, "Review of *Bloodlands: Europe between Hitler and Stalin* by Timothy Snyder," *Slavic Review* 70, no. 2 (2011): 427.

5   John Connelly, "Gentle Revisionism," in "Review Forum: Timothy Snyder, *Bloodlands: Europe between Hitler and Stalin*," by John Connelly et al., *Journal of Genocide Research* 13, no. 3 (2011): 320.

6   Zbigniew Truchlewski, "Timothy Snyder, A Historian of Eastern Europe," *Nouvelle Europe [en ligne]*, February 11, 2013, accessed February 25, 2016, http://www.nouvelle-europe.eu/node/1640.

7   On area studies, see for example the following recent reports on *H-Soz-Kult*: "Area Studies in the 21st Century / Eastern Europe Without Borders, 09.11.2015—10.11.2015 London," *H-Soz-Kult*, 7 November 2015, accessed February 29, 2016, http://www.hsozkult.de/event/id/termine-29443; "Podiumsdiskussion: Vom Nutzen der area studies in Zeiten der Globalisierung, 12.11.2015 Berlin," *H-Soz-Kult*, November 4, 2015, accessed February 29, 2016, http://www.hsozkult.de/event/id/termine-29418. On Snyder's participation in a recent conference focusing on Ukraine, see "Tagungsbericht: Revolution und Krieg. Die Ukraine in den großen Transformationen des neuzeitlichen Europa. Konferenz der Deutsch-Ukrainischen Historikerkommission, 28.05.2015 – 29.05.2015 Berlin," *H-Soz-Kult*, November 9, 2015, accessed February 29, 2016, http://www.hsozkult.de/conferencereport/id/tagungsberichte-6234.

8 David Mikics, "The Diplomat of Shoah History: Does Yale Historian Timothy Snyder Absolve Eastern Europe of Special Complicity in the Holocaust?" *Tablet*, July 26, 2012, accessed February 25, 2016, http://www.tabletmag. com/jewish-arts-and-culture/books/107382/diplomat-of-shoah-history.

9 See for example Artur Komilienko, "Snyder's 'Bloodlands' Released in Russian Despite Deadlock to Publish in Russia," *Kyiv Post*, July 13, 2015, accessed February 25, 2016, www.kyivpost.com/content/ukraine/snyders-bloodlands-released-in-russian-despite-deadlock-to-publish-in-russia-393339. html; Cathrin Kahlweit, "'Bloodlands' erscheint auf russisch—in der Ukraine," *Süddeutsche Zeitung*, July 18, 2015, accessed February 25, 2016, http://www.sueddeutsche.de/politik/timothy-snyder-wie-zur-zeit-des-samisdat-1.2565450.

10 See the summary of praise in David Herman, "Why *Bloodlands* is Still One of the Books of the Year," *New Statesman*, October 3, 2010, accessed February 25, 2016, http://www.newstatesman.com/blogs/cultural-capital/2010/12/soviet-snyder-history-europe.

11 See for instance the controversy aroused by his most recent monograph: Timothy Snyder, *Black Earth: The Holocaust as History and Warning* (London: Bodley Head, 2015).

12 See for example Daniel Lazare, "Timothy Snyder's Lies," *Jacobin*, September 9, 2014, accessed February 25, 2016, https://www.jacobinmag. com/2014/09/timothy-snyders-lies/.

13 *Economist, The*, eds., "History and its Woes: How Stalin and Hitler Enabled Each Other's Crimes," *The Economist,* October 14, 2010; accessed February 25, 2016, http://www.economist.com/node/17249038.

14 Grover Furr, *Blood Lies: The Evidence That Every Accusation Against Joseph Stalin and the Soviet Union in Timothy Snyder's Bloodlands Is False* (New York: Red Star Publishers, 2014).

15 *Economist, The*, eds., "History and its Woes."

MODULE 8
PLACE IN THE AUTHOR'S WORK

KEY POINTS

- Much of Snyder's work has been characterized by an interest in Poland and Ukraine, whether in national or geographical terms.

- Although Snyder's previous books include both microhistorical* biographies (histories written from the perspective of specific individuals) and large-scale national histories, his body of work is generally united by a focus on the individuality of historical actors and their fates.

- *Bloodlands* made Timothy Snyder's reputation as a public intellectual and political commentator, as well as enhancing his academic standing worldwide.

Positioning

Timothy Snyder's *Bloodlands: Europe Between Hitler and Stalin* has been widely hailed as the work of a historian at the height of his powers: a grand, groundbreaking synthesis, based on years of archival and secondary research, and interpreting sources in a whole plethora of Central European languages. However, Snyder had previously cut his scholarly teeth on a series of biographies that were far more narrowly focused. These included the book based on his PhD thesis, a study of a Polish scholar and political philosopher entitled *Nationalism, Marxism, and Modern Central Europe: A Biography of Kazimierz Kelles-Krauz* * (1998), as well as a biography of the Polish statesman and intelligence operative Henryk Józewski,* entitled *Sketches from a Secret War: A Polish Artist's Mission to Liberate Soviet Ukraine* (2005), and a biography of former Archduke Wilhelm von Habsburg,* entitled *The Red Prince: The Fall of a Dynasty and the Rise of Modern Europe* (2008).[1]

> **❝** Bloodlands is a big, macro[historical]* book
> because it contains the questions which I felt it was
> my responsibility to try to answer. In that sense it's a
> different book, much less personal than the other books,
> or if it's personal, it's more personal in an intellectual
> way. It's about the questions that East European
> historians and the historians of Europe in general have
> to answer and could now try to answer because of all
> of the research being done and all of the sources being
> opened in the East in the last twenty years ... **❞**
>
> Timothy Snyder, in Zbigniew Truchlewski, "Timothy Snyder, A Historian of
> Eastern Europe," *Nouvelle Europe*

Meanwhile, a more wide-ranging scholarly work, *The Reconstruction of Nations: Poland, Ukraine, Lithuania, Belarus, 1569–1999* (2003), explored nation-building and mythmaking in Poland, Ukraine, Lithuania, and Belarus over the course of four centuries.[2] To varying degrees, all of these works reflected Snyder's burgeoning interest in the construction of Polish and Ukrainian nationalism*—a political ideology based on notions of national superiority—that also gradually began to betray itself in his contributions to debates on current affairs and post-Cold War* memory politics[3] (politics in which the memory of national grievances, hardship, achievements, and so on, are used as a foundation for modern political movements).

However, Snyder has commented that "over the course of writing four other books that were about nationalism ... I came to the conclusion that national history, however pluralistic or critical or reflective, was inadequate to the history of Eastern Europe in the twentieth century."[4] As his interest in the causes of the Holocaust* grew, he began to develop transnational* ideas about the genocide that would foreground some of the arguments put forward in

Bloodlands—while still concentrating on Poland and Ukraine in geographical terms.[5]

Meanwhile, *Bloodlands* itself can now be seen to have paved the way for Snyder's latest major work, *Black Earth: The Holocaust as History and Warning* (2015), which also focuses on the lawless killing fields of Eastern Europe, rather than on the death factories of the concentration camps.*[6]

Integration

At first glance, the major texts in Snyder's body of work might seem strikingly diffuse, with nothing more than a vaguely Central or Eastern European location to bind them together. What, after all, could unify a Holocaust blockbuster such as *Bloodlands* with three autobiographies of rather obscure central European figures, and with an in-depth study of Polish, Lithuanian, Ukrainian, and Belorussian nationalisms? Here, however, Snyder himself has a convincing answer: "If you just do biography or micro-history, you can forget about the larger structures. If you just do the history of the largest structures, you can forget about the significance of the individual ... Doing both is a way not to forget the dilemma of being a historian ... Even in *Bloodlands*, I do try to make a point making sure that we remember that everyone to whom these events happened is an individual. That's the significance of history ..."[7]

Although *The Reconstruction of Nations* is primarily concerned with national history over the *longue durée* (a historical term simply meaning "a long period of time"), and the three biographies focus more exclusively on individual microhistories, each work shares with *Bloodlands* a concern with the ideological motivations of human actors, especially in nationalist terms.[8] Moreover, along with some of Snyder's most seminal articles, many of his books, including *Bloodlands*, represent an attempt to illuminate the causes of ethnic cleansing.*[9] In sum, as the Israeli historian Dan Diner* has pointed out, in *Bloodlands*

Snyder's explorations of the "conflict-ridden relationship between layers of ethnic and social belonging are clearly enmeshed in a constellation carefully explored in [his] previous research."[10]

Significance

To date, *Bloodlands* is undoubtedly Snyder's most important book—although his new blockbuster ecological interpretation of the Holocaust,* *Black Earth*, currently looks set to stir up even more controversy.[11] Snyder's earlier works, particularly his biographies, had certainly attracted a significant amount of popular as well as academic acclaim, receiving a good smattering of reviews in the quality press,[12] and *The Reconstruction of Nations* was also awarded a number of prizes.[13] However, none of these books could match the phenomenal reception of *Bloodlands*, both in terms of worldwide success and ever-expanding—if at times heatedly controversial—debate. As the US historian Walter Laqueur* has put it in a recent reassessment of Snyder's work, "No author of books on Eastern Europe during the period of World War II* and the Holocaust has been more widely reviewed and discussed in recent years than Timothy Snyder."[14]

While critics had previously gone out of their way to stress the sophistication, or even the poetic nature, of Snyder's literary style—often praising his learning, mastery of multiple languages, and scholarly acumen[15]—*Bloodlands* was instantly hailed as a tour de force, in which all of these virtues were writ large for a popular audience. Indeed, as one reviewer pointed out in an article defending the book against its critics, "The *Atlantic,* the *Independent,* the *Telegraph,* and the [*Financial Times*] joined … the *New Statesman*, in choosing *Bloodlands* as one of the books of the year."[16]

Furthermore, as the US author Daniel Lazare* has noted, "*Bloodlands* catapulted Snyder into the top rungs of punditdom, winning him a coveted spot as a regular contributor to the *New York Review of Books*."[17] Indeed, Snyder has since established himself as a notable commentator on politics and current affairs, with a particular—though not exclusive—focus on events in Eastern Europe in general, and Ukraine in particular.[18] From this perspective, the success of *Bloodlands* has been crucial in cementing Snyder's position not merely as a successful academic, but as a high-profile public intellectual.

NOTES

1   Timothy Snyder, *Nationalism, Marxism, and Modern Central Europe: A Biography of Kazimierz Kelles-Krauz (1872–1905)* (Cambridge, MA: Harvard University Press, 1998); Timothy Snyder, *Sketches from a Secret War: A Polish Artist's Mission to Liberate Soviet Ukraine* (New Haven: Yale University Press, 2005); Timothy Snyder, *The Red Prince: The Fall of a Dynasty and the Rise of Modern Europe* (London: Bodley Head, 2008).

2   Timothy Snyder, *The Reconstruction of Nations: Poland, Ukraine, Lithuania, Belarus, 1569–1999* (New Haven: Yale University Press, 2003).

3   Timothy Snyder and Timothy Garton Ash, "The Orange Revolution," The *New York Review of Books*, April 28, 2005, represents Snyder's first major foray into commentary on current affairs. See also Timothy Snyder, "Memory of Sovereignty and Sovereignty over Memory: Poland, Lithuania and Ukraine, 1939–1999," in Jan-Werner Müller (ed.), *Memory and Power in Post-war Europe* (Cambridge: Cambridge University Press, 2004), 39–58.

4   Timothy Snyder, "The Causes of the Holocaust," *Contemporary European History* 21, no. 2 (2012): 153.

5   See Timothy Snyder, "Holocaust: The Ignored Reality," The *New York Review of Books*, July 16, 2009, accessed February 25, 2016, http://www.nybooks.com/articles/archives/2009/jul/16/holocaust-the-ignored-reality/. This is a key example of this trend.

6   Timothy Snyder, *Black Earth: The Holocaust as History and Warning* (London: Bodley Head, 2015).

7   Zbigniew Truchlewski, "Timothy Snyder, A Historian of Eastern Europe,"
      Nouvelle Europe [en ligne], February 11, 2013, accessed February 29,
      2106, http://www.nouvelle-europe.eu/node/1640.

8   Truchlewski, "Timothy Snyder."

9   Snyder's articles on this theme include Timothy Snyder, "To Resolve the
      Ukrainian Problem Once and for All: The Ethnic Cleansing of Ukrainians
      in Poland, 1943–1947," *Journal of Cold War Studies* 1, no. 2 (1999):
      86–120; "The Causes of Ukrainian-Polish Ethnic Cleansing, 1943," *Past
      & Present* 179, no. 1 (2003): 197–234; Timothy Snyder, "The Life and
      Death of Western Volhynian Jewry, 1921–1945," in *The Shoah in Ukraine:
      History, Testimony, Memorialization,* ed. Ray Brandon and Wendy Lower
      (Bloomington: Indiana University Press, 2008), 77–113.

10   Dan Diner, "Topography of Interpretation: Reviewing Timothy Snyder's
      Bloodlands," *Contemporary European History* 21, no. 2 (2012): 128.

11   For examples of recent reactions to the publication of *Black Earth* that
      stress the book's controversial nature, see Richard J. Evans, "*Black
      Earth* by Timothy Snyder: Review—A New Lesson to be Learned from
      the Holocaust," The *Guardian*, September 10, 2015, accessed February
      25, 2016, http://www.theguardian.com/books/2015/sep/10/black-earth-
      holocaust-as-history-timothy-snyder-review; Walter Laqueur, "Timothy Snyder:
      The Newton of the Holocaust?" *Mosaic*, November 4, 2015, accessed
      February 25, 2016, http://mosaicmagazine.com/observation/2015/11/
      timothy-snyder-the-newton-of-the-holocaust/; Allan Levine, "Review: *Black
      Earth*, Timothy Snyder's New Book on the Origins of the Holocaust, Is Sure
      to Spark Controversy," *Globe and Mail*, September 11, 2015, accessed
      February 25, 2016, http://www.theglobeandmail.com/arts/books-and-media/
      review-black-earth-timothy-snyders-new-book-on-the-origins-of-the-holocaust-
      is-sure-to-spark-controversy/article26333226/; Michael Pinto-Duschinsky,
      "Hitler's 'Ecological Panic' Didn't Cause the Holocaust," *Standpoint*,
      September 2015, accessed February 25, 2016, http://www.standpointmag.
      co.uk/node/6189/full.

12   Examples include Anne Applebaum, "Painter, Hero, Governor, Spy,"
      The *Spectator*, July 12, 2006, accessed February 25, 2016, http://new.
      spectator.co.uk/2006/07/painter-dreamer-governor-spy/ and Brendan
      Simms, "*The Red Prince* by Timothy Snyder: How the Dandy Turned Hero as
      Europe Burned," The *Independent*, July 11 2008, accessed February 25,
      2016, http://www.independent.co.uk/arts-entertainment/books/reviews/the-
      red-prince-by-timothy-snyder-864388.html.

13   Yale University Press, *The Reconstruction of Nations: Poland, Ukraine,
      Lithuania, Belarus*, 1569–1999 by Timothy Snyder, Yale University Press
      website, accessed March 1, 2016, http://history.yale.edu/timothy-snyder/
      reconstruction-nations-poland-ukraine-lithuana-belarus-1569-1999.

14   Laqueur, "Timothy Snyder."

15 For example: Ludomir R. Lozny, "Review of *Nationalism, Marxism and Modern Central Europe: A Biography of Kazimierz Kelles-Krauz (1872–1905)* by Timothy Snyder," *Canadian Slavonic Papers / Revue Canadienne des Slavistes* 42, no. 3 (2000): 369–71; John-Paul Himka, "Review of *The Reconstruction of Nations: Poland, Ukraine, Lithuania, Belarus, 1569–1999* by Timothy Snyder," *American Historical Review* 109, no. 1 (2004): 280; Jeremy King, "Review of *The Red Prince: The Secret Lives of a Habsburg Archduke* by Timothy Snyder," *Slavic Review* 68, no. 3 (2009): 665–6.

16 David Herman, "Why *Bloodlands* is Still One of the Books of the Year," *New Statesman*, October 3, 2010, accessed February 25, 2016, http://www. newstatesman.com/blogs/cultural-capital/2010/12/soviet-snyder-history-europe.

17 Daniel Lazare, "Timothy Snyder's Lies," *Jacobin*, September 9, 2014, accessed February 25, 2016, https://www.jacobinmag.com/2014/09/timothy-snyders-lies/.

18 For some examples, see Timothy Snyder, "Beneath the Hypocrisy, Putin is Vulnerable. Here's Where His Soft Spots Are," *New Republic*, March 2, 2014, accessed February 25, 2016, https://newrepublic.com/article/116812/how-europe-should-respond-russian-intervention-ukraine; Timothy Snyder, "Far-Right Forces are Influencing Russia's Actions in Crimea," *New Republic*, March 17, 2014, accessed February 25, 2016, https://newrepublic.com/article/117048/far-right-forces-are-influencing-russias-actions-crimea; Timothy Snyder, "Putin's New Nostalgia," The *New York Review of Books*, November 10, 2014, accessed February 25, 2016, http://www.nybooks.com/blogs/nyrblog/2014/nov/10/putin-nostalgia-stalin-hitler/.

SECTION 3
IMPACT

MODULE 9
THE FIRST RESPONSES

KEY POINTS

- *Bloodlands* has divided reviewers; although it has received an immense amount of acclaim, some aspects of the book have also been heavily criticized.

- Snyder has been keen to respond to his critics, and to correct what he feels are misconceptions of his work.

- Snyder has generally stood by the claims that he made in Bloodlands, while addressing some of the concerns raised by critics in his new book, *Black Earth*.

Criticism

Timothy Snyder's *Bloodlands: Europe Between Hitler and Stalin* is arguably one of the most popular, energetically debated and divisive works to have recently appeared in modern European history.[1] From one perspective, the book's appearance was a triumph—*Bloodlands* won numerous Book of the Year awards, was translated into a wide range of languages, and gained fulsome praise from pundits and the quality press, as well as from many of Snyder's academic colleagues.[2] The historian of Eastern Europe Anne Applebaum,* writing in the *New York Review of Books*, lauded *Bloodlands* as "a brave and original history of mass killing in the twentieth century,"[3] while Neal Ascherson, the reviewer for the *Guardian* newspaper, deemed Snyder "a noble writer as well as a great researcher."[4]

Nevertheless, there certainly exist other spheres of public and academic opinion whose attitudes toward *Bloodlands* were not quite so generous. Often, scholars with a close connection to Snyder's topic pointed out what they saw as flaws or even politicized biases in his

> ❝ Snyder's book is revisionist history of the best kind:
> in spare, closely argued prose, with meticulous use of
> statistics, he makes the reader rethink some of the best-
> known episodes in Europe's modern history. For those
> who are wedded to the simplistic schoolbook notions
> that the Hitlerites were the mass murderers and the
> Soviets the liberators, or that the killing started in 1939
> and ended in 1945, Mr. Snyder's theses will be thought
> provoking or shocking ... Some ghastly but well-known
> episodes recede; others emerge from the shadows. ❞
>
> *The Economist*, "History and its Woes: How Stalin and Hitler Enabled Each
> Other's Crimes"

arguments and his narrative. Some critics, most trenchantly the
historian Richard J. Evans* in the *London Review of Books*, claimed
that "by focusing exclusively on what he calls the 'bloodlands', Snyder
also demeans, trivializes or ignores the suffering of the many other
Europeans who were unfortunate enough to fall into Nazi* hands."[5]
In this context, the British historian Mark Mazower* suggested that
Snyder's approach to mass killing could have been more comparative,
situating the "bloodlands" within a broader landscape of the
"borderlands zone of genocide* [that the historians] Mark Levene,*
Aviel Roshwald* and others have seen as stretching from the Baltic
through the Black Sea* to Anatolia* and the Mediterranean."[6] The
Holocaust scholar Doris Bergen* also questioned Snyder's exclusion
of other important areas of mass killing from the "bloodlands,"
including Yugoslavia* (a state now dissolved into the nations of Bosnia
and Herzegovina, Montenegro, Macedonia, Croatia, Slovenia, and
Serbia), and Transnistria* (the area lying between the Eastern
European river Dniester and the eastern Ukrainian border.)[7]

Bergen also raised another key factor that has reappeared countless times in criticisms of *Bloodlands*: Snyder's "emphasis … on imported violence" at the expense of treating local collaboration.*[8] As one reviewer in *Times Higher Education* put it, "In his portrait of the region, Snyder is keen to emphasize widespread suffering, including interethnic cooperation among Jewish* and non-Jewish victims of Nazi rule. Correspondingly, he downplays … the indigenous Jew-hatred and local reasons for collaboration that historian Jan Gross* has heroically brought to light."[9]

Responses

Snyder has never been backward in coming forward when it comes to defending his work against his critics. He has participated in several roundtable issues of scholarly journals, including *Contemporary European History* and the *Journal of Genocide Research*, all of which have brought him face to face with hostile reviewers.[10] He is also keen to correct what he deems to be misconceptions of his work by publishing articles in the media, such as his "In Defense of *Bloodlands*," which appeared in the *Tablet* magazine.[11]

Although Snyder is not often prepared to change his stance, at times he is prepared to make common ground with some of his critics. For instance, in a roundtable review organized by the online discussion network H-Diplo, Snyder justified his treatment of the collaboration issue in response to Christopher Browning's* criticisms, while at the same time stressing how much he agreed with Browning on certain points, such as the importance of ideology.[12]

However, the repeated criticisms related to the failure of *Bloodlands* to treat collaboration comprehensively could also raise Snyder's hackles; in the review forum organized by the *Journal of Genocide Research*, he commented stridently that "unlike my critics on this point, I have devoted a great deal of attention to precisely the issue of East European collaboration with occupying forces, using East European languages … to do so. I was among those who introduced into Western historiography* the single major example of non-state-led ethnic cleansing,* the mass murder of Poles* by Ukrainian* nationalists ..."[13]

Conflict and Consensus

Snyder's responses to criticism can occasionally be rather violent—witness his rather personal responses to the German historian Thomas Kühne's* review essay ("almost every reader and reviewer aside from Kühne has understood [the] point that we must write new and better history ... unhindered by the [Historians' Dispute]".)*[14] In particular, he denigrates critics such as Kühne and the Israeli historian Efraim Zuroff,* whom he considers as belonging to "a kind of nationalist international," and who must therefore be deeply opposed to *Bloodlands* on ideological grounds.[15]

In some senses, he conceives of the book as providing a crucial defense against national history's "powerful hold on the imagination" and against "[the] tempting and frequent conflation of the national and the principled."[16] From this perspective, it is hardly surprising that he has not chosen to revise his opinions significantly in the light of such criticisms, particularly given the lavish praise that the book has received in other quarters.

Nor have Snyder's critics often relented in their views; frequently, those who were skeptical about the content of *Bloodlands* have revealed themselves to be equally, if not more, skeptical about the claims of his latest book, *Black Earth: The Holocaust as History and Warning* (2015). To take one example, the British historian Richard J. Evans, reviewing *Black Earth* in the *Guardian*, commented, "*Black Earth* shares some of the same failings as that flawed work [*Bloodlands*], delivering an account of the Holocaust that is skewed far too much towards eastern Europe."[17] However, it is worth noting that Snyder has included in *Black Earth* an entire chapter on Eastern European collaborationism—arguably a response to those who bemoaned the topic's lack of treatment in *Bloodlands*. "Collaborationism" is a term describing the way in which citizens of nations conquered by the Nazi regime collaborated with it in committing crimes against humanity.

NOTES

1   Walter Laqueur, "Timothy Snyder: The Newton of the Holocaust?" *Mosaic*, November 4, 2015, accessed February 25, 2016, http://mosaicmagazine. com/observation/2015/11/timothy-snyder-the-newton-of-the-holocaust/.

2   For examples, see Zina Gimpelvich, "Review of *Bloodlands: Europe between Hitler and Stalin* by Timothy Snyder," *Canadian Slavonic Papers/Revue Canadienne des Slavistes* 53, no. 2/4 (2011): 634–6; David Herman, "Review of *Bloodlands: Europe between Hitler and Stalin* by Timothy Snyder," *New Statesman*, November 30, 2010, accessed February 25, 2016, http://www.newstatesman.com/books/2010/11/million-soviet-snyder-europe; David Herman, "Why *Bloodlands* is Still One of the Books of the Year," *New Statesman*, October 3, 2010, accessed February 25, 2016, http://www.newstatesman.com/blogs/cultural-capital/2010/12/ soviet-snyder-history-europe; Justin McCauley, "Book Review: Timothy Snyder's *Bloodlands*," The *Vienna Review*, May 20, 2012, accessed February 25, 2016, http://www.viennareview.net/vienna-review-book-reviews/ book-reviews/it-tolls-for-thee; Ian Thomson, "Review of *Bloodlands: Europe between Hitler and Stalin* by Timothy Snyder," The *Telegraph*, November 9, 2010, accessed February 25, 2016, http://www.telegraph.co.uk/culture/ books/bookreviews/8120244/Bloodlands-Europe-Between-Hitler-and-Stalin-review.html.

3   Anne Applebaum, "The Worst of the Madness," The *New York Review of Books*, November 11, 2010, accessed February 25, 2016, http://www. nybooks.com/articles/2010/11/11/worst-madness/.

4   Neal Ascherson, "Review of *Bloodlands: Europe between Hitler and Stalin* by Timothy Snyder," The *Guardian*, October 9, 2010, accessed March 1, 2016, http://www.theguardian.com/books/2010/oct/09/bloodlands-stalin-timothy-snyder-review.

5   Richard J. Evans, "Who Remembers the Poles?" *London Review of Books*, November 4, 2010, accessed February 25, 2016, http://www.lrb.co.uk/ v32/n21/richard-j-evans/who-remembers-the-poles. The ensuing letters to the editor raised the point that Evans might have been particularly

hostile to Snyder's work because of Snyder's earlier harsh critique of Evans's own book on the Third Reich at war—see further Timothy Snyder, "Nazis, Soviets, Poles, Jews," The *New York Review of Books*, December 3, 2009, accessed February 25, 2016, http://www.nybooks.com/articles/archives/2009/dec/03/nazis-soviets-poles-jews/#fnr1-316546747, reviewing Richard J. Evans, *The Third Reich at War: How the Nazis Led Germany from Conquest to Disaster* (London: Penguin, 2009), and the subsequent debate in Richard J. Evans, "Nazis, Soviets, Poles, Jews: An Exchange," The *New York Review of Books*, February 11, 2010, accessed February 25, 2016, http://www.nybooks.com/articles/2010/02/11/nazis-soviets-poles-jews-an-exchange/.

6   Mark Mazower, "Timothy Snyder's *Bloodlands*," *Contemporary European History* 21, no. 2: 121. See further Mark Levene, *Genocide in the Age of the Nation-State*, 2 vols. (London: Routledge, 2005); Aviel Roshwald, *Ethnic Nationalism and the Fall of Empires: Central Europe, Russia and the Middle East, 1914–1923* (London: Routledge, 2001).

7   Doris L. Bergen, "'The Loneliness of the Dying': General and Particular Victimization in Timothy Snyder's *Bloodlands: Europe between Hitler and Stalin*," *Journal of Modern Russian History and Historiography* 4 (2011): 214–15. In general terms, Bergen's article gives an excellent historiographical overview of the context of Snyder's work.

8   Bergen, "Loneliness of the Dying," 216.

9   *Times Higher Education*, eds. "Review of *Bloodlands: Europe between Hitler and Stalin* by Timothy Snyder." *Times Higher Education*, January 27, 2011, accessed February 25, 2016, https://www.timeshighereducation.com/books/bloodlands-europe-between-hitler-and-stalin/414946.article. The anonymous reviewer is referring in particular to Jan Gross's *Neighbors: The Destruction of the Jewish Community in Jedwabne, Poland* (Princeton: Princeton University Press, 2001).

10   *Contemporary European History* 21, no. 2 (2012); John Connelly et al., "Review Forum: Timothy Snyder, *Bloodlands: Europe between Hitler and Stalin*," *Journal of Genocide Research* 13, no. 3 (2011): 313–52; "H-Diplo Roundtable Review of Timothy Snyder, *Bloodlands: Europe between Hitler and Stalin*," *H-Diplo Roundtable Reviews* 13, no. 2 (2011); Christian Ingrao et al., "Comment écrire l'histoire de l'Europe des massacres?" *Le Débat: histoire, politique, société* 172, no. 5 (2012), 152–92.

11   Timothy Snyder, "In Defense of *Bloodlands*," *Tablet*, August 3, 2012, accessed February 25, 2016, http://www.tabletmag.com/jewish-arts-and-culture/books/108229/in-defense-of-bloodlands.

12   "H-Diplo Roundtable Review of Timothy Snyder, *Bloodlands: Europe between Hitler and Stalin*," 23–4.

13 Timothy Snyder, "Collaboration in the Bloodlands," *Journal of Genocide Research* 13, no. 3 (2011): 347.

14 Timothy Snyder, "The Causes of the Holocaust," *Contemporary European History* 21, no. 2 (2012): 157.

15 Snyder, "Causes of the Holocaust," 156, n. 11.

16 Snyder, "Causes of the Holocaust," 151. See also Donald A. Yerxa, "*Bloodlands: Europe between Hitler and Stalin*: An Interview with Timothy Snyder," *Historically Speaking* 12, no. 5 (2011): 30.

17 Richard J. Evans, "*Black Earth* by Timothy Snyder: Review—A New Lesson to be Learned from the Holocaust," The *Guardian*, September 10, 2015, accessed February 25, 2016, http://www.theguardian.com/books/2015/sep/10/black-earth-holocaust-as-history-timothy-snyder-review.

MODULE 10
THE EVOLVING DEBATE

KEY POINTS

- *Bloodlands* has recently been put to deliberate use in identity politics in the region on the border of Europe and Asia known as the South Caucasus* and other parts of Eastern Europe; "identity politics" describes political activism conducted by people claiming membership of a specific group.

- Academic discussion of *Bloodlands* has been intense; the book has also raised hackles among a group of scholars and commentators, chief among them the American Lithuanian scholar Dovid Katz,* who accuse Snyder of fostering Holocaust* revisionism (a challenge to the historical consensus, in this case seeking to lessen the crimes of the Holocaust).

- The concept of "bloodlands" is now used as a term by scholars in a variety of disciplines, as are a number of other concepts that were popularized by Snyder in the book.

Uses And Problems

One of the most influential uses of Timothy Snyder's *Bloodlands: Europe Between Hitler and Stalin* has been the fostering of various forms of identity politics in the nations of Eastern Europe on which the book's narration centers. As the English literature scholar David Mikics* has argued, "Bloodlands has been translated into Polish, Ukrainian, and Lithuanian, and when readers from those countries read the book, they are forced to reckon with the enormity of the Holocaust."[1]

> ❝ The goal of the project implemented in June–October 2014 was to publish ... *Bloodlands* in Georgian. In discussing the atrocities committed in the 'bloodlands' by both Stalin* and Hitler,* readers will connect Hitler's politically motivated killing as part of the same historical phenomenon as the violence perpetrated by Stalin. In a country where ... 45 percent of the population holds a positive view of Stalin and 68 percent would characterize him as a 'wise leader,' a book that ... details the millions who died under his rule and ... compares this violence to that of Nazi Germany, would spark a much needed reappraisal of Georgia's infamous son. ❞
>
> Heinrich Böll Foundation South Caucasus, "Rethinking Stalinist History through the publication of Timothy Snyder's *Bloodlands: Europe Between Hitler and Stalin* (2014)"

One recent example of this trend can be found in the nation of Georgia,* where the first Georgian translation of *Bloodlands* was published in 2014 by the Henrich Böll Foundation (an independent political organization with ecological concerns). The report on the Foundation's website states that the publication was accompanied by numerous events throughout the country "in order to empower ordinary Georgian citizens and stakeholders by engaging them with an unfamiliar interpretation of this period in Soviet* history."[2]

Mikics has also noted that *Bloodlands* can have a transformative effect on Jewish attitudes: "When Jews* read *Bloodlands*, they are challenged to acknowledge the struggles of other groups, the mass death that afflicted them, too. We are reminded that everyone's fate is interlocked with everyone else's. This is one reason—a fitting, even necessary one—for writing, as Snyder does, about all the murdered peoples of the bloodlands together."[3]

Schools of Thought

It is fair to say that *Bloodlands* has not yet spawned any particular academic school of thought, though Snyder has certainly been successful in redirecting attention toward the history of Eastern Europe, and in making a case for the importance of writing wide-ranging transnational* histories of Europe's dark twentieth century. Nevertheless, Snyder's ideas have been very influential, both academically and politically, since the book's publication.

One indication of this is the number of journal special issues and roundtable reviews that have been devoted to *Bloodlands*,[4] as well as the number of lengthy review essays that treat the work prominently. The Holocaust scholar Doris Bergen's* article in the *Journal of Modern Russian History and Historiography*, Dovid Katz's contribution in *East European Jewish Affairs*, the German historian Michael Wildt's* extended essay in the journal *Kritika*, and the German historian Jürgen Zarusky's* article in the contemporary history journal *Vierteljahrshefte für Zeitgeschichte* are all excellent examples of this trend.[5] Scholars working on this area and period may not all be convinced by Snyder's ideas, but they still need to take them seriously into account.

If anything, Snyder's harshest critics could be said to have set up a sort of "anti-Snyderian" school of thought, rebuking him for fostering pro-Polish and pro-Ukrainian nationalist sentiments that unthinkingly equate Stalinist* and Nazi* atrocities, and downplay Eastern Europeans' own anti-Semitism* and the contribution they made to the Holocaust by collaborating with the occupying Nazi regime. The best evidence of such stances can be found on the website run by Dovid Katz, *defendinghistory.com*, which features headlines such as "Defending Holocaust History Against the New Revisionism: Reviews of Timothy Snyder's *Black Earth*," and "Daniel Lazare Deconstructs Timothy Snyder's Trashing of Anti-Nazi World War II

Partisans, and New Role as Point Man for (East European) Far Right and (US) Neo-Cons."[6] "Neo-cons"—short for neo-conservatives—refers to a strand of right-wing politics in the United States in which American interests are to be aggressively prioritized, even through military force if required.

In Current Scholarship

That Snyder's coinage "bloodlands" has already become a useful term in scholarly literature on Eastern Europe and World War II,* even in the few years since the book was first published, is indisputable. The word has become a convenient shorthand for scholars in a whole range of disciplines—not just for historians, but also for sociologists* or even musicologists. In an article on "Hearing the Holocaust in Soviet Jewish Culture," James Loeffler* comments that "of late, historians have begun to shift their collective gaze eastward, from the confines of Auschwitz* to the 'bloodlands' of Ukraine."[7]

Similarly, in an article for *Critical Enquiry* that analyzes Snyder's work alongside that of the cartoonist Art Spiegelman* and others, the legal scholar Norman Spaulding* takes over Snyder's terminology unquestioningly: "Even in the most mnemonically barren landscapes of the bloodlands, even in improvised mass graves, people survived to testify."[8] By "mnemonically barren landscapes," he describes a place in which the memory of massacre is quite lost.

The scholar of Baltic history Anu Mai Köll* has also noted the importance of the "bloodlands" concept as an interpretative framework in her study of Soviet peasant persecution in the Baltic state of Estonia,* as well as engaging with one of the key questions posed in *Bloodlands*: How, in retrospect, can the war experience be incorporated in the narrative of Soviet terror?[9] Meanwhile, other scholars have engaged with the careful use of terminology that Snyder puts forward in *Bloodlands*, preferring to use the term "mass killing" instead of genocide,* "in order to include ... cases in which the victims were selected on grounds other than ethnic or racial ones."[10]

Perhaps one of the greatest tributes to Snyder's crucial contribution is the recent publication of an edited volume entitled *Reconciliation in Bloodlands: Assessing Actions and Outcomes in Contemporary Central-Eastern Europe.*[11] The editor and contributors confess their debt to Snyder's coinage in the introduction to the book, even though they believe it necessary to extend its geographical focus: "In our title we refer to the title of [Snyder's book], though we think the scope of [the] European Bloodlands is larger than he thought." Rather, they envisage the "bloodlands" as stretching from the Baltic Sea* in the North to the Black Sea* and the Adriatic* in the South.[12] What better example could there be of the ways in which current scholars are constantly working with—and expanding upon—the ideas that Snyder first put forward in his greatest work to date?

NOTES

1   David Mikics, "The Diplomat of Shoah History: Does Yale Historian Timothy Snyder Absolve Eastern Europe of Special Complicity in the Holocaust?" *Tablet*, July 26, 2012, accessed February 25, 2016, http://www.tabletmag. com/jewish-arts-and-culture/books/107382/diplomat-of-shoah-history.

2   Heinrich Böll Foundation South Caucasus, "Rethinking Stalinist History Through the Publication of Timothy Snyder's *Bloodlands: Europe Between Hitler and Stalin* (2014)," September 27, 2014, accessed February 25, 2016, https://ge.boell.org/en/2014/09/27/rethinking-stalinist-history-through-publication-timothy-snyders-bloodlands-europe.

3   Mikics, "The Diplomat of Shoah History." This, however, is also the reason why some Jewish critics were rather less than enamored of *Bloodlands*: see for example Alexander J. Groth, "Review of *Bloodlands: Europe between Hitler and Stalin* by Timothy Snyder," *Israel Journal of Foreign Affairs* 5, no. 2 (2011): 123–28; Robert Rozett, "Diminishing the Holocaust: Scholarly Fodder for a Discourse of Distortion," *Israel Journal of Foreign Affairs* 6, no. 1 (2012): 53–64.

4   *Contemporary European History* 21, no. 2 (2012); John Connelly et al.,
    "Review Forum: Timothy Snyder, Bloodlands: Europe between Hitler and
    Stalin," *Journal of Genocide Research* 13, no. 3 (2011): 313–52; "H-Diplo
    Roundtable Review of Timothy Snyder, *Bloodlands: Europe between Hitler
    and Stalin*," *H-Diplo Roundtable Reviews* 13, no. 2 (2011); Christian Ingrao
    et al., "Comment écrire l'histoire de l'Europe des massacres?" *Le Débat:
    histoire, politique, société* 172, no. 5 (2012), 152–92.

5   Doris L. Bergen, "'The Loneliness of the Dying': General and Particular
    Victimization in Timothy Snyder's *Bloodlands: Europe between Hitler and
    Stalin*," *Journal of Modern Russian History and Historiography* 4 (2011):
    206–22; Dovid Katz, "Detonation of the Holocaust in 1941: A Tale of Two
    Books," *East European Jewish Affairs* 41, no. 3 (2011): 207–21; Michael
    Wildt, "Review of *Bloodlands: Europe between Hitler and Stalin* by Timothy
    Snyder," *Kritika: Explorations in Russian and Eurasian History* 14, no.
    1 (2013): 197–206; Jürgen Zarusky, "Timothy Snyder's 'Bloodlands':
    Kritische Anmerkungen zur Konstruktion einer Geschichtslandschaft,"
    Vierteljahrshefte für Zeitgeschichte 60, no. 1 (2012): 1–31. See also
    Jacques Sémelin, "Snyder and his Critics," books&ideas.net, February 14,
    2013, accessed March 1, 2016, http://www.booksandideas.net/Timothy-
    Snyder-and-his-Critics.html; Rozett, "Diminishing the Holocaust."

6   http://defendinghistory.com/—accessed March 1, 2016.

7   James Loeffler, "'In Memory of our Murdered (Jewish) Children': Hearing the
    Holocaust in Soviet Jewish Culture," *Slavic Review* 73, no. 3 (2014): 588.

8   Norman W. Spaulding, "Resistance, Countermemory, Justice," *Critical
    Enquiry* 41, no. 1 (2014): 144.

9   Anu Mai Köll, *The Village and the Class War: Anti-Kulak Campaign in Estonia
    1944–49* (Budapest: Central European University Press, 2013), 233, 252.

10 Antonio Ferrara, "Eugene Kulischer, Joseph Schechtman and the
    Historiography of European Forced Migrations," *Journal of Contemporary
    History* 46, no. 4 (2011): 739.

11 Jacek Kurczewski, ed. *Reconciliation in Bloodlands: Assessing Actions and
    Outcomes in Contemporary Central-Eastern Europe* (Oxford: Peter Lang,
    2014).

12 Kurczewski, *Reconciliation in Bloodlands*, 8.

MODULE 11
IMPACT AND INFLUENCE TODAY

KEY POINTS

- Since it was first published in 2010, *Bloodlands* has become a classic of twentieth-century European popular history.

- *Bloodlands* has been condemned particularly harshly by pro-Russian commentators, while being greeted in Ukraine as a welcome corrective to the current pro-Stalinist* historical narrative offered by Russia.

- *Bloodlands* has also been criticized for playing into the hands of Eastern European ultranationalists (activists whose right-wing politics are founded on ideas of nationhood) who are keen to equate Nazi* and Soviet* crimes so that their countries' participation in the Holocaust* will be lost in the greater narrative of their nation's unique suffering.

Position

Since its publication in 2010, Timothy Snyder's *Bloodlands: Europe Between Hitler and Stalin* has set the agenda for academic, public, and political debates about Nazi and Soviet atrocities, World War II,* and the Holocaust. The book seems set to become a classic, and has already run into multiple editions, as well as having been "translated into 35 languages between 2010 and 2014."[1] The publication of Snyder's next book on the Holocaust, *Black Earth: The Holocaust as History and Warning*, has recently ensured the beginning of a new round of debate on the merits and demerits of *Bloodlands* as well.[2]

Bloodlands has certainly aroused both hostility and admiration among certain sections of its readership. First, Snyder's conclusions

> ❝ Some of the negative comments on Snyder are highly emotional and even personal to a degree unusual in historical debate. He has been accused of prevarication, of consorting with shady characters in the present-day Baltic republics, of deliberately downplaying anti-Semitism and the unique character of the Final Solution, of anti-Russian and pro-Polish bias, and more. Skeptical reviewers in Europe have focused on his alleged espousal of the "double- genocide" theme—that is, equating the scale and seriousness of the atrocities committed respectively by Hitler* and Stalin. ❞
>
> Walter Laqueur, "Timothy Snyder: The Newton of the Holocaust?" *Mosaic*

have been forcefully criticized by commentators on the left of the political spectrum who are known to have pro-Russian, pro-Putin* or pro-Communist* leanings ("Putin" here refers to the Russian head of state Vladimir Putin). Foremost among these is the historian Grover Furr* of the United States, a trenchant defender of the Soviet leader Joseph Stalin whose strongly worded criticisms of Snyder's comparison of Nazi and Soviet crimes (both in print and online) repeatedly claim that "virtually everything Snyder has to say about Soviet history of this period is false," including his account of the Ukrainian famine (the Holodomor),* and the Soviet–Nazi non-aggression pact of August 1939—the Molotov-Ribbentrop Pact.*[3] Meanwhile, the left-wing journalist and commentator Daniel Lazare* has condemned Snyder for peddling "a dangerous farrago of half-truths and non-sequiturs"— indeed, his extremely critical review essay of *Bloodlands* for *Jacobin* magazine was actually entitled "Timothy Snyder's Lies."[4]

Interaction

Bloodlands arguably poses a particular danger to pro-Russian sentiment in the present day because of its damning condemnation of Stalin's crimes against humanity. In present-day Ukraine, the book provides what one commentator has termed "a powerful intellectual alternative to Russia's official historical discourse and propaganda," particularly at a time when the Ukraine has been "suffering from Russian aggression."[5] Although the book had been prevented from publication in Russia, a Ukrainian press finally brought out the first Russian-language edition, which was then distributed free to schools, libraries, and other civil organizations.[6]

Bloodlands has not only posed challenges for Russians and pro-Russian commentators, however. It has also been used as a tool by politicians and right-wing movements in the Baltic states* and Ukraine, as part of a European Union*-sponsored reconciliation initiative that highlights the monstrosity of both Nazi and Soviet crimes.[7] As the US author Menachem Kaiser* has pointed out, "A few, but a very vocal few, [have] accused Snyder of being complicit (or of being an unprotesting accessory) in what they have coined the 'double genocide' theory.* This theory posits that in several Eastern European countries … certain ultranationalist individuals, groups, and/or institutions are pushing for further inquiry into and exposure of Soviet crimes as a means to downplay the severity of their own crimes against their Jewish* populations … *Bloodlands*, according to at least one critic, has become their 'Bible'."[8]

The Continuing Debate

In protest at what they see as Snyder's witting or unwitting endorsement of the "double genocide" thesis, in which Eastern European nations have called on the European Union to recognize Communism and Nazism as a common legacy, commentators such as the American Lithuanian scholar Dovid Katz* have criticized Snyder very harshly.[9] For instance, Katz himself has gone so far as to accuse Snyder of contributing to what he calls "Holocaust Obfuscation," because of the "unfortunate, if coincidental, congruence of ... *Bloodlands* with the [image] of history currently promoted via ample investment by a number of right-wing governments and political forces in Eastern Europe."[10] In contrast with the US-based historian Alexander Prusin,* whose book *The Lands Between: Conflict in the East European Borderlands, 1870–1992* was published in the same year as *Bloodlands*, these critics see Snyder as providing an "inexplicable free(ish) pass ... to the local perpetrators (particularly those in Lithuania, Latvia, Estonia and Ukraine) [who were] plain and simple, *killers.*"[11]

Even the Berlin-based historian Grzegorz Rossolinski-Liebe,* who is ready to admit Snyder's critical stance toward nationalism* and ultranationalism alike, criticizes the fact that "Poles in *Bloodlands* mainly appear as victims of other regimes and only very marginally as perpetrators. This narrative is in total agreement with how Polish 'patriots' imagine the history of the Second World War, but it is in contradiction with what history as an academic discipline has to say ..."[12]

In similar vein, contributors to *Defending History* (a website founded with the aim of protecting the historical importance of the Holocaust from Holocaust revisionism),* such as the German political scientist Clemens Heni,* have strongly criticized Snyder for his "comparative trivizalization" of the Holocaust.[13] With the publication of *Black Earth*, these debates seem set to continue—even if in altered form—now that Snyder has put forward "ecological" interpretations of the Holocaust that some of his critics have found even harder to swallow.[14]

NOTES

1 Michael Pinto-Duschinsky, "Hitler's 'Ecological Panic' Didn't Cause the Holocaust," *Standpoint*, September 2015, accessed February 25, 2016, http://www.standpointmag.co.uk/node/6189/full.

2 See for example the reviews by David Frum, "Beyond the Bloodlands," *Commentary*, November 1, 2015, accessed February 25, 2016, https://www.commentarymagazine.com/articles/beyond-the-bloodlands/; Walter Laqueur, "Timothy Snyder: The Newton of the Holocaust?" *Mosaic*, November 4, 2015, accessed February 25, 2016, http://mosaicmagazine.com/observation/2015/11/timothy-snyder-the-newton-of-the-holocaust/; Richard J. Evans, "*Black Earth* by Timothy Snyder: Review—A New Lesson to be Learned from the Holocaust," The *Guardian*, September 10, 2015, accessed February 25, 2016, http://www.theguardian.com/books/2015/sep/10/black-earth-holocaust-as-history-timothy-snyder-review; Allan Levine, "Review: *Black Earth*, Timothy Snyder's New Book on the Origins of the Holocaust, Is Sure to Spark Controversy," The *Globe and Mail*, September 11, 2015, accessed February 25, 2016, http://www.theglobeandmail.com/arts/books-and-media/review-black-earth-timothy-snyders-new-book-on-the-origins-of-the-holocaust-is-sure-to-spark-controversy/article26333226/; Dieter Pohl, "Review of *Black Earth: The Holocaust as History and Warning* by Timothy Snyder," *H-Soz-Kult*, 15 October 2015, accessed February 25, 2016, http://www.hsozkult.de/publicationreview/id/rezbuecher-24652.

3 Grover Furr, "I Protest the Appearance of Professor Timothy Snyder!" April 18, 2012, accessed November 2015, https://msuweb.montclair.edu/~furrg/research/timothy_snyder_protest_0412.html; see also Grover Furr, *Blood Lies: The Evidence That Every Accusation Against Joseph Stalin and the Soviet Union in Timothy Snyder's* Bloodlands *Is False* (New York: Red Star Publishers, 2014). On the importance of the Holodomor for Ukrainian national identity, see Alexander J. Motyl, "Deleting the Holodomor: Ukraine Unmakes Itself," *World Affairs* 173, no. 3 (2010), 25–34.

4 Daniel Lazare, "Timothy Snyder Does It Again," daniellazare.com, November 12, 2014, accessed February 25, 2016, http://daniellazare.com/2014/11/12/timothy-snyder-does-it-again/; Daniel Lazare, "Timothy Snyder's Lies," *Jacobin*, September 9, 2014, accessed February 25, 2016, https://www.jacobinmag.com/2014/09/timothy-snyders-lies/.

5 Artur Komilenko, "Snyder's 'Bloodlands' Released in Russian Despite Deadlock to Publish in Russia," *Kyiv Post*, July 13, 2015, accessed February 25, 2016, www.kyivpost.com/content/ukraine/snyders-bloodlands-released-in-russian-despite-deadlock-to-publish-in-russia-393339.html; see also Cathrin Kahlweit, "'Bloodlands' erscheint auf russisch — in der Ukraine," *Süddeutsche Zeitung*, July 18, 2015, accessed February 25, 2016, http://www.sueddeutsche.de/politik/timothy-snyder-wie-zur-zeit-des-samisdat-1.2565450.

6   Komilienko, "Deadlock."

7   See further Grzegorz Rossolinski-Liebe, "Debating, Obfuscating and Disciplining the Holocaust: Post-Soviet Historical Discourses on the OUN-UPA and Other Nationalist Movements," *East European Jewish Affairs* 42, no. 3 (2012): 199–241, for discussion and a comprehensive bibliography.

8   Menachem Kaiser, "Unshared Histories: Timothy Snyder's 'Bloodlands'," *Los Angeles Review of Books*, October 16, 2012, accessed February 25, 2016, https://lareviewofbooks.org/review/unshared-histories-timothy-snyders-bloodlands.

9   Dovid Katz, "Detonation of the Holocaust in 1941: A Tale of Two Books," *East European Jewish Affairs* 41, no. 3 (2011): 207–21; Dovid Katz, "Why Red is not Brown in the Baltics: Unhappily, Timothy Snyder's Historical Reassessment of the Nazi-Soviet Pact Coincides with Baltic Ultra-nationalist Agendas," The *Guardian*, September 30, 2010, accessed February 25, 2016, http://www.theguardian.com/commentisfree/cifamerica/2010/sep/30/baltic-nazi-soviet-snyder; Dovid Katz, "An Open Letter to Yale History Professor Timothy Snyder," *Algemeiner*, May 21, 2012, accessed February 25, 2016, http://www.algemeiner.com/2012/05/21/an-open-letter-to-yale-history-professor-timothy-snyder/#; see also Jonathan Freedland, "I See Why 'Double Genocide' Is a Term Lithuanians Want. But It Appalls Me," The *Guardian*, September 14, 2010, accessed February 25, 2016, http://www.theguardian.com/commentisfree/2010/sep/14/double-genocide-lithuania-holocaust-communism and, more generally, the website www.defendinghistory.com.

10 Katz, "Detonation of the Holocaust in 1941," 210.

11 Katz, "Detonation of the Holocaust in 1941," 210; see also Robert Rozett, "Diminishing the Holocaust: Scholarly Fodder for a Discourse of Distortion," *Israel Journal of Foreign Affairs* 6, no. 1 (2012): 61; Alexander V. Prusin, *The Lands Between: Conflict in the East European Borderlands, 1870–1992* (Oxford: Oxford University Press, 2010).

12 Rossolinski-Liebe, "Debating, Obfuscating and Disciplining the Holocaust," 226.

13 Clemens Heni, "Ernst Nolte's Grandson," Defending History.com, accessed February 25, 2016, http://defendinghistory.com/ernst-noltes-grandson/39530.

14 See for example Pinto-Duschinsky, "Hitler's 'Ecological Panic' Didn't Cause the Holocaust."

MODULE 12
WHERE NEXT?

KEY POINTS

- Some scholars have argued that *Bloodlands* is at the forefront of a new wave of scholarship that seeks to find similarities between the Holocaust* and other acts of mass killing, rather than stressing its uniqueness.

- Snyder has suggested that future research on the "bloodlands" could greatly benefit from detailed local studies that engage with sources in multiple languages.

- *Bloodlands* provides us with a whole range of new intellectual frameworks for considering Eastern European experiences of the twentieth century.

Potential

Timothy Snyder's *Bloodlands: Europe Between Hitler and Stalin* (2010) seems likely to stay at the forefront of debate on the place of the Holocaust within European history for some time to come—and not only because Snyder's new book, *Black Earth: The Holocaust as History and Warning* (2015), has drawn renewed attention to his previous work on the topic. For instance, in an article published in 2015 in the *Journal of Genocide Research*, the Israeli scholar Daniel Blatman* has argued that *Bloodlands* is in the vanguard of a new wave of Holocaust scholarship, a "post-uniqueness era," in which scholars do not shy away from comparing the Shoah* with other forms of genocide.*[1] Blatman argues that "the great challenge raised by Snyder is the attempt to explain the Nazis'* murder of the Jews* as one thread of a historical narrative that integrates parameters that have not been extensively used in Holocaust studies: time, space, territory and the mutual

> ❝Timothy Snyder's *Bloodlands* has given a strong boost to scholars wishing to study Stalinism* and Nazism as transnational rather than as comparative history. What future scholars can do to build on his monumental work is to develop the systemic dimension to the mode of inquiry he has done so much to promote.❞
>
> Michael David-Fox, "Entanglements, Dictators and Systems," *Journal of Genocide Research*

influences of ideologies."[2]

Snyder himself has suggested that the arguments put forward in *Bloodlands* might be helpful in the attempt to create a more united form of "European identity" in the face of nationalist hostility to the European Union:* "[To] solve the broader European question of why there was so much ethnic cleansing*... there will have to be some way of producing European history, which can then be taught at the elementary and secondary school level, not at the university level because it's too late ..."[3] He also thinks it possible that, if Russian politics were to shift significantly, common views and approaches between Russia and its neighboring nations could be fostered in connection with the history of the "bloodlands."[4]

Future Directions

Snyder himself has suggested a number of future directions that scholars could take—or are already taking—that could build on his work in *Bloodlands*. In a roundtable debate that appeared in the *Journal of Genocide Research* in 2011, he declared that "we need much more work by scholars using both local languages and German sources."[5] In this context, he has praised the work of the Canada-based historian John-Paul Himka* on the role of Ukrainian nationalists in anti-Semitic* violence, and the study of the Final Solution* in the Latvian city of Riga* by Andrej Angrick,*[6] an expert on the Holocaust in the Soviet Union.*

Meanwhile, in an interview he has argued that "the future of [this] kind of research is in local studies which look at both the Soviet and the German occupations,"[7] singling out recent books by the European scholars Tanja Penter* on the Ukrainian city of Donetsk* and Felix Ackermann* on Grodno* as excellent examples of what he has in mind.[8] Finally, Snyder suggests that "Double or even triple collaboration* should be looked at much more closely. That would allow us to understand better the importance of ideology in the entire process instead of always taking it for granted, which is sometimes a way to look at it very abstractly. This type of study would allow us to write a kind of grounded transnational* history, instead of a history that is transnational because it looks at people and things that move around."[9]

Summary

Bloodlands is a book of grand scope and original ambition. It encourages us to think across nations rather than within them, escaping the confines of national histories in order to think collectively and comparatively. It demands that we turn our gaze from the familiar sites of the Holocaust, especially Auschwitz,* to the barbaric killing fields of the East, and that we shift our perspective from Western Europe toward Eastern Europe. It challenges traditional narratives of victimhood, helping us to gain sympathy for groups whose suffering has more often been overlooked. In so doing, it provides a corrective to views that insist that the Final Solution was a crime so incomparable that it must forever stand outside history. It attempts instead to find a means of comparison that illuminates the less well known (yet still horrific) crimes of Stalinism* without trivializing the Holocaust. That Snyder has caused controversy in taking such a stance has only enriched academic debate rather than impoverished it, providing numerous disciplines with both fresh concepts and fruitful fodder for further scholarship. For anyone working on World War II,* the Holocaust, or the history of Europe's dark twentieth century in general, Snyder's book, and in particular his definition of the "bloodlands" that give the work its title, will be indispensable.

NOTES

1   Daniel Blatman, "Holocaust Scholarship: Towards a Post-Uniqueness Era," *Journal of Genocide Research* 17, no. 1 (2015), 21–43.

2   Blatman, "Holocaust Scholarship," 37.

3   Zbigniew Truchlewski, "Timothy Snyder, A Historian of Eastern Europe," *Nouvelle Europe [en ligne]*, February 11, 2013, accessed February 25, 2016, http://www.nouvelle-europe.eu/node/1640.

4   Radio Free Europe, "Historian Timothy Snyder: 'History is Always Plural,'" Radio Free Europe/Radio Liberty, June 20, 2015, accessed February 25, 2016, http://www.rferl.org/content/russia-ukraine-interview-bloodlands-timothy-snyder-history/27082683.html.

5   Timothy Snyder, "Collaboration in the Bloodlands," *Journal of Genocide Research* 13, no. 3 (2011): 351.

6   John-Paul Himka, "The Lviv Pogrom of 1941: The Germans, Ukrainian Nationalists, and the Carnival Crowd," *Canadian Slavonic Papers/Revue Canadienne des Slavistes* 53, no. 2/4 (2011): 209–43; Andrej Angrick and Peter Klein, *The "Final Solution" in Riga: Exploitation and Annihilation, 1941–1944* (New York: Berghahn Books, 2009).

7   Thomas Grillot and Jacques Sémelin, "A Decent and True Understanding of the Past: An Interview with Timothy D. Snyder," books& ideas.net, February 14, 2013, accessed February 25, 2016, http://www.booksandideas.net/A-Decent-and-True-Understanding-of.html.

8   Tanja Penter, *Kohle für Stalin und Hitler: Arbeiten und Leben im Donbass, 1929 bis 1953* (Essen, Klartext Verlag, 2010); Felix Ackermann, *Palimpsest Grodno: Nationalisierung, Nivellierung und Sowjetisierung einer mitteleuropäischen Stadt 1919–1991* (Wiesbaden, Harrassowitz Verlag, 2010).

9   Grillot and Sémelin, "A Decent and True Understanding of the Past."

GLOSSARY

GLOSSARY OF TERMS

Adriatic Sea: the part of the Mediterranean Sea that divides the east coast of Italy from the Balkans.

Anatolia: the western peninsula of the Asian continent—known as Asia Minor—that comprises most of the state of Turkey.

Anti-Semitism: hatred or prejudice against Jews.

Area studies: a field of research drawing on the knowledge and methods of different disciplines that focuses on the culture, history, and geography of a particular region.

Auschwitz: a system of labor and extermination camps run by the Nazi regime in occupied Poland. More than one million prisoners, most of them Jewish, died in the gas chambers of Auschwitz–Birkenau.

Baltic Sea: part of the Atlantic Ocean, surrounded by Scandinavia, Finland, and the Baltic States.

Baltic states: the countries of Estonia, Latvia, and Lithuania.

Black Sea: a tideless, inland sea connected to the Mediterranean, surrounded by Ukraine, Russia, Georgia, Turkey, Bulgaria, and Romania.

Buczacz: a town in western Ukraine, situated on the River Strypa.

Cold War: the state of political hostility between the communist countries of the Eastern bloc, led by Soviet Russia, and the Western powers, led by the United States, that existed between 1945 and 1990.

Collaboration: treacherous cooperation with enemy forces during a military occupation.

Communism: a revolutionary ideology that advocates class war and common ownership of property. In communist dictatorships, the state tends to control all aspects of society.

Concentration camp: a punitive camp in which large numbers of people are interned, especially political prisoners or persecuted minorities. Inmates are often made to perform forced labor, or they may be imprisoned until their execution.

Darwinism: Charles Darwin's theory of the evolution of species through natural selection.

Donetsk: a Ukrainian industrial city, situated on the River Kalmius.

Double genocide theory: the idea that the crimes committed by the Soviet Union are equal to the Holocaust in terms of their genocidal atrocity.

Eastern bloc: the term used in the West for the formerly communist countries of Central and Eastern Europe, including the Soviet Union.

Enlightenment: a movement in late seventeenth- and eighteenth-century Europe that emphasized the use of reason to increase knowledge and improve society.

Ethnic cleansing: the systematic expulsion of members of an ethnic or religious group from their territory by force.

European Union: political-economic union of 28 states, whose members are primarily in Europe. It was established by six founding members—Belgium, France, West Germany, Italy, Luxembourg, and the Netherlands—in 1957.

Final Solution: the Nazi regime's policy of systematic extermination of the European Jews, which resulted in the Holocaust.

French Revolution: a period of radical social change in France that took place between 1789 and 1799, resulting in the abolition of the French monarchy and the establishment of a secular, democratic republic.

Generalplan Ost: Hitler's secret plan for the colonization of Eastern Europe and the enslavement or genocide of the Slavic peoples.

Genocide: mass killing of a group of people, particularly on ethnic grounds.

Georgia: a former Soviet Socialist Republic in the Caucasus region of Eurasia.

Grodno: a city in Belarus that lies near the Polish and Lithuanian borders.

Historikerstreit (Historians' dispute): a debate that took place among German historians in 1986–87, in which a group of conservative historians, including Ernst Nolte, demanded a "normalization" and "relativization" of Nazi crimes and of the Holocaust.

Historiography: writing about history, or the study of how a historical debate evolves over time

Holocaust: the mass murder of approximately six million Jews by the Nazi regime between 1941 and 1945.

Holocaust revisionism: attempts to revise the usual historical narrative of the Holocaust, or to claim that the deaths caused were far less numerous than the accepted statistic of six million.

Holodomor: the Ukrainian famine, or "extermination by hunger," that took place in 1932–33. It formed part of a widespread famine caused by Stalin's demographic and agricultural policies in the Soviet Union, and resulted in the starvation of several million Ukrainians.

Iron Curtain: the notional boundary separating communist Eastern Europe from Western Europe in the period between 1945 and 1991.

Jews: An ethno-religious group related to the ancient Hebrews. Throughout the centuries, they have often been subject to extreme prejudice.

Macrohistory: a form of historical writing that focuses on long-standing trends, patterns, and processes within world history.

Microhistory: a form of history that challenges the generalizations that are often made in traditional forms of social history, focusing instead on a single event, individual, or community.

Molotov–Ribbentrop line: the line dividing Romania, Poland, the Baltic states, and Finland into German and Soviet spheres of influence, as agreed in the Molotov–Ribbentrop Pact.

Molotov–Ribbentrop Pact: a treaty of nonaggression that was signed between Nazi Germany and Soviet Russia on August 23, 1939, by Soviet foreign minister Vyacheslav Molotov and German foreign minister Joachim von Ribbentrop.

Napoleonic Wars: a series of wars fought by Napoleon I and the French Empire against a number of other European powers, including Great Britain and Prussia, between 1803 and 1815.

Nationalism: a belief in the primacy of the nation-state, or in the superiority of one's own country at the expense of others.

National Socialism/Nazism: the far-right ideology put forward by Hitler and the National Socialist German Workers' Party (NSDAP). Key traits include racism, anti-Semitism, and German nationalism.

Polonocentric: focused on Poland; treating Poland as of central importance.

Red Army: the name given to the armed forces of the Soviet Union.

Riga: the capital city of Latvia, one of the Baltic states.

Serbs: an ethnic group of South Slavs (a subgroup of the Slavic peoples), native to the Balkans, predominantly Orthodox Christians.

Shoah: an alternative name for the destruction of the Jews in the Holocaust.

Solidarity (*Solidarność*): a Polish nongovernment trade union movement that spearheaded resistance against the Soviet regime in Poland from 1980 onwards, and ultimately contributed to the end of communist rule.

South Caucasus: the region that lies between Eastern Europe and Southwest Asia, including Armenia, and much of Georgia and Azerbaijan.

Soviet Union (USSR): the Union of Soviet Socialist Republics was a communist state that encompassed Russia and its surrounding states in Eastern Europe and central Asia. The Soviet regime lasted from 1922 until 1991.

Stalinism: the form of communism propounded by Joseph Stalin during his dictatorship over the Soviet Union, characterized in particular by state terror, suppression of dissidents, and a totalitarian state apparatus.

Third Reich: a term for Germany between 1933 and 1945, when it was ruled by Hitler and the National Socialist regime.

Totalitarian: a regime in which the state intrusively intervenes in the life of the citizen and dissent is suppressed.

Totalitarianism theory: a theory that argues for equivalence between fascist and communist dictatorships, focusing on similarities in ideology, the presence of a one-party state, a state terror apparatus, a state monopoly on violence and mass communication, and centralized decision-making.

Transnationalism: an approach to history that tries to make connections between different countries, rather than focusing on individual nation-states. It first gained popularity in the 2000s.

Transnistria: the area lying between the River Dniester and the eastern Ukrainian border.

Wehrmacht: the name given to the armed forces of the Third Reich.

World War II: a global war that involved all of the world's great powers and numerous other countries around the globe. The war resulted in an estimated 50–85 million deaths. Its outbreak was motivated by Hitler's desire to conquer an empire across Europe and western Russia that would equal the United States.

Yugoslavia: a country in the Balkans that existed from 1918 until 1991. Its territory included Bosnia and Herzegovina, Croatia, Macedonia, Montenegro, Slovenia, and Serbia.

PEOPLE MENTIONED IN THE TEXT

Felix Ackermann is visiting DAAD associate professor for applied humanities at the European Humanities University in Vilnius, Lithuania. He is the author of *Palimpsest Grodno: Nationalisierung, Nivellierung und Soujetisierung einer mitteleuropäischen Stadt 1919–1991* (2010).

Andrej Angrick (b. 1962) is an expert on the Holocaust in the Soviet Union. He has been closely affiliated with the Hamburg Institute for Social Research, especially its project on the crimes of the Wehrmacht.

Anne Applebaum (b. 1964) is a journalist and a historian of Russia and Eastern Europe. She won the Pulitzer Prize for her history of the Soviet camp system, *Gulag: A History* (2003). Her latest book is entitled *Iron Curtain: The Crushing of Eastern Europe 1944–1956* (2012).

Hannah Arendt (1906–75) was a German Jewish philosopher and political theorist. In 1941 she immigrated to the United States, playing a key part in American intellectual life. Her most famous works include *The Origins of Totalitarianism* (1951) *and Eichmann in Jerusalem: A Report on the Banality of Evil* (1963).

Neal Ascherson (b. 1932) is a Scottish journalist and writer, a historian with a particular interest in Poland and Eastern Europe.

Timothy Garton Ash (b. 1955) is professor of European studies at Oxford University. He is a historian, author, and political commentator, best known for his work on the contemporary history of Central and Eastern Europe.

Jörg Baberowski (b. 1961) is a German historian, an expert on Stalinism, particularly Stalinist terror. He is professor of Eastern European history at Humboldt University, Berlin.

Omer Bartov (b. 1954) is a professor of history and German studies at Brown University. He is an expert on World War II and the Holocaust, particularly focusing on the barbarization of warfare in Eastern Europe.

Doris Bergen is the Chancellor Rose and Ray Wolfe Professor of Holocaust Studies at the University of Toronto. She is an expert on religion, gender, and ethnicity during the Holocaust and World War II.

Karel C. Berkhoff (b. 1965) is a senior researcher at the NIOD Institute for War, Holocaust and Genocide Studies, part of the Royal Netherlands Academy of Arts and Sciences. He is best known for his book *Harvest of Despair: Life and Death in Ukraine under Nazi Rule (2004).*

Daniel Blatman is professor of modern Jewish history and Holocaust studies at the Hebrew University of Jerusalem. He is best known for his work on the Holocaust, especially his book *The Death Marches: The Final Phase of Nazi Genocide* (2011).

Ray Brandon is a freelance translator, historian, and researcher based in Berlin. He is also a former editor at the English edition of the *Frankfurter Allgemeine Zeitung*.

Christopher Browning (b. 1944) is an American historian and emeritus professor at the University of North Carolina. He is best known for his work on the Holocaust and its perpetrators, and in particular for his book *Ordinary Men: Reserve Police Battalion 101 and the Final Solution in Poland* (1992).

Alan Bullock (1914–2004) was a British historian and the founding master of St Catherine's College, Oxford. He made his name with his biography of Hitler, titled *Hitler, A Study in Tyranny* (1952).

John Connelly (b. 1959) is an American historian and a professor at UC Berkeley. His research interests include modern Eastern and Central European political and social history, particularly communism.

Robert Conquest (1917–2015) was a British American historian and poet. He was one of the greatest experts on Soviet Russia and the Stalinist terror.

Norman Davies (b. 1939) is a British historian, writer, and political commentator. His research has focused primarily on the history of Poland and Eastern Europe.

Dan Diner (b. 1946) is a historian and professor at the Hebrew University of Jerusalem. He has written numerous books on Nazism and the legacies of the Holocaust in politics and memory.

Richard J. Evans (b. 1947) is the former regius professor of history at the University of Cambridge, and is the president of Wolfson College. His most famous work is his best-selling *Third Reich Trilogy*. In 2012 he was knighted for services to scholarship.

Saul Friedländer (b. 1932) is the author of a two-volume history of Nazi Germany and the Jews and is one of the world's leading experts on the Holocaust. He is currently a professor at UCLA.

François Furet (1927–97) was a French historian, best known for his work on the French Revolution, as well as for his book *The Passing of an Illusion: The Idea of Communism in the Twentieth Century* (1995).

Grover Furr (b. 1944) is a revisionist historian of Russia, and particularly Stalinism. He is also a professor of medieval English literature at Montclair State University in the United States.

Robert Gellately (b. 1943) is a Canadian historian and a professor of history at Florida State University. He made his name with his research on the Gestapo and the Nazi terror system.

Christian Gerlach (b. 1963) is a professor of history at the University of Bern. He is best known for his work on the Holocaust and extreme violence in modern societies.

Mary Gluck is professor of history and comparative literature at Brown University. She specializes in the intellectual and cultural history of Central Europe and France.

Daniel Jonah Goldhagen (b. 1959) is an American author, formerly based at Harvard University. He gained worldwide renown with his highly controversial book *Hitler's Willing Executioners: Ordinary Germans and the Holocaust* (1996), which argued that Germans had always had an inborn tendency to hate and destroy Jews.

Jan Gross (b. 1947) is professor of war and society and professor of history at Princeton University. His unflinching and meticulously researched studies of Polish anti-Semitic atrocities, particularly *Neighbors: The Destruction of the Jewish Community in Jedwabne, Poland* (2000) have caused great controversy in Poland, his home country.

Wilhelm von Habsburg (1895–1948) was a Habsburg archduke, an officer in the Austrian army, a playboy, and would-be king of Ukraine. He was heavily involved in Ukrainian nation-building during the interwar period.

Clemens Heni (b. 1970) is a German political scientist, author, and public intellectual. He is the director of the Berlin International Center for the Study of Anti-Semitism.

Raul Hilberg (1926–2007) was an Austrian Jewish historian who spent most of his adult life in the United States, having fled Nazism with his family. His three-volume work *The Destruction of the European Jews* established him as one of the world's greatest authorities on the Holocaust.

John-Paul Himka (b. 1949) is an emeritus professor at the University of Alberta, Canada. He is an expert on Slavic and Ukrainian history.

Heinrich Himmler (1900–45) was Reich Leader of the SS from 1929 to 1945. He was primarily responsible for the Holocaust, and by the early 1940s had gained power over much of the apparatus of the Nazi state. He was one of Hitler's most trusted henchmen.

Adolf Hitler (1889–1945) was the leader of the National Socialist (Nazi) Party, and Chancellor of Germany between 1933 and 1945. He ruled the Third Reich as a fascist dictatorship, and was responsible for millions of deaths caused by World War II and the Holocaust, which he instigated.

Christian Ingrao (b. 1970) is the director of France's *Institut de l'histoire du temps present* (Institute for Contemporary History). He is best known for his work on the SS and Nazi genocide.

Jerzy Jedlicki (b. 1930) is a Polish historian and professor. He specializes in Polish cultural and social history from the eighteenth century to the present.

Henryk Józewski (1892–1981) was a Polish artist and politician. He served in the Polish resistance during World War II.

Tony Judt (1948–2010) was a British historian of Europe, and the founder and director of the Remarque Institute at New York University. He is best known for his book *Postwar: A History of Europe Since 1945* (2005), and for his political and historical essays in periodicals such as the *New York Review of Books*.

Menachem Kaiser (b. 1985) is a Brooklyn-based Jewish author, critic, and journalist; he recently held a Fulbright fellowship based in Lithuania. He regularly contributes to publications such as the *Wall Street Journal*, *The Atlantic*, *Slate*, *Tablet*, and *Vogue*.

Dovid Katz (b. 1956) is an American Lithuanian scholar. He is an expert on Lithuanian Jewry and Yiddish linguistics, as well as a human rights activist.

Kazimierz Kelles-Krauz (1872–1905) was a Polish Marxist, sociologist, and philosopher. He was also arguably one of the first thinkers to engage with the study of nationalism as it is conceived today.

Anu Mai Köll is professor emerita of Baltic history, culture, and society at Södertörn University, Sweden. Her research interests include Swedish and Baltic agrarian history, economic history, and the history of Soviet repression in the Baltic States.

Thomas Kühne is a German historian, and professor of history and Holocaust studies at Clark University. He is particularly known for his work on mass violence and genocide.

Walter Laqueur (b. 1921) is a Jewish American historian, and a commentator on current affairs. He is an expert on nineteenth- and twentieth-century European history.

Daniel Lazare is an American author and journalist. His books include *The Velvet Coup: The Constitution, the Supreme Court, and the Decline of American Democracy* (2001).

Mark Levene (b. 1953) is a reader in history at the University of Southampton. He specializes in the history of genocide and in modern Jewish history.

James Loeffler is an associate professor at the University of Virginia. His books include *The Most Musical Nation: Jews and Culture in the Late Russian Empire* (2010).

Peter Longerich (b. 1955) is director of the Research Center for the Holocaust and Twentieth-Century History at Royal Holloway, University of London. He is one of the world's leading experts on Nazi Germany and the Holocaust.

Mark Mazower (b. 1958) is professor of history at Columbia University. He has written numerous best selling histories of twentieth-century Europe, including *Dark Continent: Europe's Twentieth Century* (1998) *and Hitler's Empire: Nazi Rule in Occupied Europe* (2008).

David Mikics (b. 1961) is professor of English at Houston University, as well as being an author, critic, and columnist. His books include *Slow Reading in a Hurried Age* (2013).

Norman Naimark (b. 1944) is professor of history and East European studies at Stanford University. He is particularly known for his work on Russian history, and on ethnic cleansing in twentieth-century Europe.

Ernst Nolte (b. 1923) is one of Germany's most notorious historians of the twentieth century. He courted controversy with his revisionist argument that the Holocaust was a response to the threat of Bolshevism, and that Hitler might have had rational reasons for attacking the Jews.

Richard Overy (b. 1947) is a British historian and a professor of history at the University of Exeter. His research interests include the history of the Nazi and Stalinist dictatorships, and World War II. His best selling books include *Why the Allies Won* (1995) and *The Dictators* (2004).

Tanja Penter (b. 1967) is professor of Eastern European history at the University of Heidelberg. She is an expert on the history of Nazism and Stalinism in comparative perspective, and on the Holocaust.

Dieter Pohl (b. 1964) is a German historian and a professor at the University of Klagenfurt. He specializes in Nazi and Soviet history.

Vladimir Putin (b. 1952) has been the president of Russia since 2012. He was also president between 2000 and 2008, as well as serving as Russian prime minister in 1999–2000 and 2008–12. Previously, he was an officer in the KGB, the Soviet intelligence service.

Alexander Prusin is an associate professor of history at the New Mexico Institute of Mining and Technology. He is best known for his book *The Lands Between: Conflict in the East European Borderlands 1870–1992* (2010).

Aviel Roshwald (b. 1962) is a professor of history at Georgetown University. He is an expert in the history of nationalism, particularly in Central Europe and the Middle East.

Grzegorz Rossolinski-Liebe (b. 1979) is currently a research fellow at the department of history and cultural studies at the Free University, Berlin. He is best known for his work on Ukrainian nationalism.

Norman W. Spaulding (b. 1971) is Nelson Bowman Sweitzer and Marie B. Sweitzer Professor of Law at Stanford Law School. He has a particular interest in law and the humanities.

Art Spiegelman (b. 1948) is a Jewish American cartoonist. He won critical and popular acclaim for his graphic novel *Maus: A Survivor's Tale* (1980), which depicts the sufferings of his family in the Holocaust.

Joseph Stalin (1878–1953) was the leader of the Soviet Union's communist dictatorship from the 1920s until his death in 1953. Under his rule, many millions of people died, either at his orders, or due to his agricultural policies that caused widespread famine.

Christian Streit is a German historian. He is best known for his work on the mistreatment of Soviet prisoners-of-war by the Nazis.

Lynne Viola (b. 1955) is a professor at the University of Toronto. She is an expert on the political and social history of twentieth-century Russia.

Piotr Wandycz (b. 1923) is a Polish American historian, and an emeritus professor at Yale University. He is best known for his work on Eastern and Central European history, particularly during the twentieth century.

Nicolas Werth (b. 1950) is a French expert on communism. He has written numerous works on the history of the Soviet Union.

Michael Wildt (b. 1954) is professor of German history at the Humboldt University in Berlin. He is best known for his work on the perpetrators of the Holocaust.

Jürgen Zarusky (b. 1958) is a German historian based at the Institute for Contemporary History in Munich. He is best known for his work on comparative totalitarianism.

Efraim Zuroff (b. 1948) is an Israeli historian who has been instrumental in bringing Nazi war criminals to justice. He is the director of the Simon Wiesenthal Center in Jerusalem.

WORKS CITED

WORKS CITED

Ackermann, Felix. *Palimpsest Grodno: Nationalisierung, Nivellierung und Sowjetisierung einer mitteleuropäischen Stadt 1919–1991.* Wiesbaden, Harrassowitz Verlag, 2010.

Angrick, Andrej. *Besatzungspolitik und Massenmord: Die Einsatzgruppe D in der südlichen Sowjetunion 1941–1943.* Hamburg: Hamburger Edition, 2003.

Angrick, Andrej, and Peter Klein. *The "Final Solution" in Riga: Exploitation and Annihilation, 1941–1944.* Translated by Ray Brandon. New York: Berghahn Books, 2009.

Applebaum, Anne. "Painter, Hero, Governor, Spy." *The Spectator,* July 12, 2006. Accessed February 25, 2016. http://new.spectator.co.uk/2006/07/painter-dreamer-governor-spy/.

———. "The Worst of the Madness." *New York Review of Books,* November 11, 2010. Accessed February 25, 2016. http://www.nybooks.com/articles/2010/11/11/worst-madness/.

Arendt, Hannah. *The Origins of Totalitarianism.* New York: Harcourt, Brace, 1951.

Ascherson, Neal. "Review of *Bloodlands: Europe between Hitler and Stalin* by Timothy Snyder." The *Guardian,* October 9, 2010. Accessed February 25, 2016. http://www.theguardian.com/books/2010/oct/09/bloodlands-stalin-timothy-snyder-review.

Baberowski, Jörg. "Once and For All: The Encounter Between Stalinism and Nazism. Critical Remarks on Timothy Snyder's *Bloodlands.*" *Contemporary European History* 21, no. 2 (2012): 145–8.

Bartov, Omer. "Eastern Europe as the Site of Genocide." *Journal of Modern History* 80, no. 3 (2008), 557–93.

———. *The Eastern Front, 1941–1945: German Troops and the Barbarization of Warfare.* Basingstoke: Palgrave Macmillan, 2001.

———. "Review of *Bloodlands: Europe between Hitler and Stalin* by Timothy Snyder." *Slavic Review* 70, no. 2 (2011): 424–8.

Bartov, Omer and Eric D. Weitz, eds. *Shatterzone of Empires: Coexistence and Violence in the German, Habsburg, Russian, and Ottoman Borderlands.* Bloomington: Indiana University Press, 2013.

Bauman, Zygmunt. *Modernity and the Holocaust.* Cambridge: Polity Press, 1989.

Bergen, Doris L. "'The Loneliness of the Dying': General and Particular Victimization in Timothy Snyder's *Bloodlands: Europe between Hitler and Stalin*." *Journal of Modern Russian History and Historiography* 4 (2011): 206–22.

Berkhoff, Karel C. *Harvest of Despair: Life and Death in Ukraine Under Nazi Rule.* Cambridge, MA: Harvard University Press, 2004.

Blatman, Daniel. "Holocaust Scholarship: Towards a Post-Uniqueness Era." *Journal of Genocide Research* 17, no. 1 (2015): 21–43.

Brandon, Ray and Wendy Lower, eds. *The Shoah in Ukraine: History, Testimony, Memorialization*. Bloomington: Indiana University Press, 2008.

Browning, Christopher. "H-Diplo Roundtable Review of Timothy Snyder, *Bloodlands: Europe between Hitler and Stalin*." *H-Diplo Roundtable Reviews* 13, no. 2 (2011), 9–12.

— — —. *Ordinary Men: Reserve Police Battalion 101 and the Final Solution in Poland*. New York: Harper Collins, 1992.

— — —. *The Origins of the Final Solution: The Evolution of Nazi Jewish Policy, September 1939–March 1942.* Lincoln: University of Nebraska Press, 2004.

Bullock, Alan. *Hitler and Stalin: Parallel Lives.* London: Fontana, 1998.

Connecticut Jewish Ledger editors. "Q & A with... Prof. Timothy Snyder: best-selling author of *Bloodlands: Europe Between Hitler and Stalin*." *Connecticut Jewish Ledger*, September 22, 2011. Accessed February 25, 2016. http://www.jewishledger.com/2011/09/q-a-with-prof-timothy-snyder-best-selling-author-of-bloodlands-europe-between-hitler-and-stalin/.

Connelly, John, "Gentle Revisionism." In "Review Forum: Timothy Snyder, *Bloodlands: Europe between Hitler and Stalin*," by John Connelly, Mark Roseman, Andriy Portnov, Michael David-Fox and Timothy Snyder. *Journal of Genocide Research* 13, no. 3 (2011): 313–52.

Conquest, Robert. *The Harvest of Sorrow: Soviet Collectivization and the Terror-Famine.* Oxford: Oxford University Press, 1986.

David-Fox, Michael. "Entanglements, Dictators and Systems." In "Review Forum: Timothy Snyder, *Bloodlands: Europe between Hitler and Stalin*," *Journal of Genocide Research* 13, no. 3 (2011): 20–7.

Davies, Norman. "The Misunderstood Victory in Europe." *New York Review of Books*, May 25, 1995. Accessed February 25, 2016. http://www.nybooks.com/articles/1995/05/25/the-misunderstood-victory-in-europe/.

Deák, István. "The Charnel Continent." *New Republic*, December 2, 2010. Accessed February 25, 2016. https://newrepublic.com/article/79084/snyder-bloodlands-hitler-stalin.

Diner, Dan. "Topography of Interpretation: Reviewing Timothy Snyder's *Bloodlands.*" *Contemporary European History* 21, no. 2 (2012): 125–31.

Duray, Dan. "Body Count: Timothy Snyder Strips the Holocaust of Theory." *Observer*, February 11, 2010. Accessed February 25, 2016. http://observer. com/2010/11/body-count-timothy-snyder-strips-the-holocaust-of-theory/.

Economist, The, editors. "History and its Woes: How Stalin and Hitler Enabled Each Other's Crimes." *The Economist,* October 14, 2010. Accessed February 25, 2016. http://www.economist.com/node/17249038.

Encyclopedia Britannica editors. "The Stalinist and Nazi Killing Machines: 5 Questions for *Bloodlands* Author Timothy Snyder." *Encyclopedia Britannica Blog.* Accessed February 25, 2016. http://blogs.britannica.com/2011/03/stalinist-nazi-killing-machine-5-questions-embloodlandsem-author-timothy-snyder/.

Evans, Richard J. " by Timothy Snyder Review—A New Lesson to be Learned from the Holocaust." *The Guardian*, September 10, 2015. Accessed February 25, 2016. http://www.theguardian.com/books/2015/sep/10/black-earth-holocaust-as-history-timothy-snyder-review.

———. *In Hitler's Shadow: West German Historians and the Attempt to Escape from the Nazi Past.* New York: Pantheon, 1989.

———. "Nazis, Soviets, Poles, Jews: An Exchange." *New York Review of Books*, February 11, 2010. Accessed February 25, 2016. http://www.nybooks. com/articles/2010/02/11/nazis-soviets-poles-jews-an-exchange/.

———. *The Third Reich at War: How the Nazis Led Germany from Conquest to Disaster.* London: Penguin, 2009.

———. "Who Remembers the Poles?" *The London Review of Books,* November 4, 2010. Accessed February 25, 2016. http://www.lrb.co.uk/v32/n21/ richard-j-evans/who-remembers-the-poles.

Ferrara, Antonio. "Eugene Kulischer, Joseph Schechtman and the Historiography of European Forced Migrations." *Journal of Contemporary History* 46, no. 4 (2011): 715–40.

Freedland, Jonathan. "I See Why 'Double Genocide' Is a Term Lithuanians Want. But It Appalls Me." The *Guardian*, September 14, 2010. Accessed February 25, 2016. http://www.theguardian.com/commentisfree/2010/sep/14/double-genocide-lithuania-holocaust-communism.

Friedlander, Henry. *The Origins of Nazi Genocide: From Euthanasia to the Final Solution.* Chapel Hill: University of North Carolina Press, 1995.

Friedländer, Saul. *Nazi Germany and the Jews: The Years of Persecution, 1933–1939,* New York: Harper Collins, 1997.

———. *The Years of Extermination: Nazi Germany and the Jews, 1939–1945.* New York: Harper Collins, 2007.

Frum, David. "Beyond the Bloodlands." *Commentary*, November 1, 2015. Accessed February 25, 2016. https://www.commentarymagazine.com/articles/beyond-the-bloodlands/.

Furr, Grover. *Blood Lies: The Evidence That Every Accusation Against Joseph Stalin and the Soviet Union in Timothy Snyder's* Bloodlands *Is False.* New York: Red Star Publishers: 2014.

— — — . "I Protest the Appearance of Professor Timothy Snyder!" April 18, 2012. Accessed February 25, 2016. https://msuweb.montclair.edu/~furrg/research/timothy_snyder_protest_0412.html.

Gellately, Robert. *Lenin, Stalin, and Hitler: The Age of Social Catastrophe.* New York: Knopf, 2007.

Gerlach, Christian. *Kalkulierte Morde: Die deutsche Wirtschafts—und Vernichtungspolitik in Weißrußland 1941 bis 1944.* Hamburg: Hamburger Edition, 1999.

Geyer, Michael and Sheila Fitzpatrick, eds. *Beyond Totalitarianism: Stalinism and Nazism Compared.* Cambridge: Cambridge University Press, 2009.

Gimpelvich, Zina. "Review of *Bloodlands: Europe between Hitler and Stalin* by Timothy Snyder." *Canadian Slavonic Papers / Revue Canadienne des Slavistes* 53, no. 2/4 (2011): 634–6.

Goldhagen, Daniel Jonah. *Hitler's Willing Executioners: Ordinary Germans and the Holocaust.* New York: Knopf, 1996.

Grillot, Thomas and Jacques Sémelin. "A Decent and True Understanding of the Past: An Interview with Timothy D. Snyder." *books & ideas.net*, February 14, 2013. Accessed February 25, 2016. http://www.booksandideas.net/A-Decent-and-True-Understanding-of.html?lang=en#nb5§.

Gross, Jan T. *Neighbors: The Destruction of the Jewish Community in Jedwabne, Poland.* Princeton: Princeton University Press, 2001.

Groth, Alexander J. "Review of *Bloodlands: Europe between Hitler and Stalin* by Timothy Snyder." *Israel Journal of Foreign Affairs* 5, no. 2 (2011): 123–8.

Hagen, Mark von. "Empires, Borderlands and Diasporas: Eurasia as Anti-Paradigm for the Post-Soviet Era." *American Historical Review* 109, no. 2 (2004): 445–68.

Heni, Clemens. "Ernst Nolte's Grandson." *Defending History.com*. August 8, 2012. Accessed February 25, 2016. http://defendinghistory.com/ernst-noltes-grandson/39530.

Heinrich Böll Foundation South Caucasus. "Rethinking Stalinist History Through the Publication of Timothy Snyder's *Bloodlands: Europe Between Hitler and Stalin* (2014)." www.ge.boell.org/en, September 27, 2014. Accessed February

25, 2016. https://ge.boell.org/en/2014/09/27/rethinking-stalinist-history-through-publication-timothy-snyders-bloodlands-europe.

Herman, David. "Review of *Bloodlands: Europe between Hitler and Stalin* by Timothy Snyder." *New Statesman*, November 30, 2010. Accessed February 25, 2016. http://www.newstatesman.com/books/2010/11/million-soviet-snyder-europe.

———. "Why *Bloodlands* is Still One of the Books of the Year." *New Statesman*, October 3, 2010. Accessed February 25, 2016. http://www.newstatesman.com/blogs/cultural-capital/2010/12/soviet-snyder-history-europe.

Hilberg, Raul. *The Destruction of the European Jews.* New Haven: Yale University Press, 1961.

Himka, John-Paul. "The Lviv Pogrom of 1941: The Germans, Ukrainian Nationalists, and the Carnival Crowd." *Canadian Slavonic Papers / Revue Canadienne des Slavistes* 53, no. 2/4 (2011): 209–43.

———. "Review of *The Reconstruction of Nations: Poland, Ukraine, Lithuania, Belarus, 1569–1999* by Timothy Snyder." *The American Historical Review* 109, no. 1 (2004): 280.

H-Soz-Kult editors. "Area Studies in the 21st Century / Eastern Europe Without Borders, 09.11.2015—10.11.2015 London." *H-Soz-Kult*, 7 November 2015. Accessed February 29, 2016. http://www.hsozkult.de/event/id/termine-29443.

———. "Podiumsdiskussion: Vom Nutzen der area studies in Zeiten der Globalisierung, 12.11.2015 Berlin." *H-Soz-Kult*, November 4, 2015. Accessed February 29, 2016. http://www.hsozkult.de/event/id/termine-29418.

———. "Tagungsbericht: Revolution und Krieg. Die Ukraine in den großen Transformationen des neuzeitlichen Europa. Konferenz der Deutsch-Ukrainischen Historikerkommission, 28.05.2015 – 29.05.2015 Berlin." *H-Soz-Kult*, November 9, 2015. Accessed February 29, 2016. http://www.hsozkult.de/conferencereport/id/tagungsberichte-6234.

Ingrao, Christian. *Believe and Destroy: Intellectuals in the SS War Machine.* Cambridge: Polity Press, 2013.

Ingrao, Christian, Pieter Lagrou, Andriy Portnov, Henry Rousso, Dariusz Stola, Annette Wieviorka, and Timothy Snyder. "Comment écrire l'histoire de l'Europe des massacres?" *Le Débat: histoire, politique, société* 172, no. 5 (2012), 152–92.

Judt, Tony, with Timothy Snyder. *Thinking the Twentieth Century.* London: Heinemann, 2012.

Kahlweit, Cathrin. "'Bloodlands' erscheint auf russisch—in der Ukraine." *Süddeutsche Zeitung*, July 18, 2015. Accessed February 25, 2016. http://www.sueddeutsche.de/politik/timothy-snyder-wie-zur-zeit-des-samisdat-1.2565450.

Kaiser, Menachem. "Unshared Histories: Timothy Snyder's 'Bloodlands'." *Los Angeles Review of Books*, October 16th, 2012. Accessed November 2015.

https://lareviewofbooks.org/review/unshared-histories-timothy-snyders-bloodlands.

Katz, Dovid. "Detonation of the Holocaust in 1941: A Tale of Two Books." *East European Jewish Affairs* 41, no. 3 (2011): 207–21.

————. "An Open Letter to Yale History Professor Timothy Snyder." *The Algemeiner*, May 21, 2012. Accessed February 25, 2016. http://www.algemeiner.com/2012/05/21/an-open-letter-to-yale-history-professor-timothy-snyder/#

————. "Why Red is not Brown in the Baltics: Unhappily, Timothy Snyder's Historical Reassessment of the Nazi-Soviet Pact Coincides with Baltic Ultra-nationalist Agendas." The *Guardian*, September 30, 2010. Accessed February 25, 2016. http://www.theguardian.com/commentisfree/cifamerica/2010/sep/30/baltic-nazi-soviet-snyder.

Kershaw, Ian and Moshe Lewin, eds. *Stalinism and Nazism: Dictatorships in Comparison.* Cambridge: Cambridge University Press, 1997.

King, Jeremy. "Review of *The Red Prince: The Secret Lives of a Habsburg Archduke* by Timothy Snyder." *Slavic Review* 68, no. 3 (2009): 665–6.

Köll, Anu Mai. *The Village and the Class War: Anti-Kulak Campaign in Estonia 1944–49.* Budapest: Central European University Press, 2013.

Komilienko, Artur. "Snyder's 'Bloodlands' Released in Russian Despite Deadlock to Publish in Russia." *Kyiv Post*, July 13, 2015. Accessed February 25, 2016. www.kyivpost.com/content/ukraine/snyders-bloodlands-released-in-russian-despite-deadlock-to-publish-in-russia-393339.html.

Kühne, Thomas. "Great Men and Large Numbers: Undertheorizing a History of Mass Killing." *Contemporary European History* 21, no. 2: 133–43.

Kurczewski, Jacek, ed. *Reconciliation in Bloodlands: Assessing Actions and Outcomes in Contemporary Central-Eastern Europe.* Oxford: Peter Lang, 2014.

Laqueur, Walter. "Timothy Snyder: The Newton of the Holocaust?" *Mosaic*, November 4, 2015. Accessed February 25, 2016. http://mosaicmagazine.com/observation/2015/11/timothy-snyder-the-newton-of-the-holocaust/.

Lazare, Daniel. "Timothy Snyder Does It Again." daniellazare.com, November 12, 2014. Accessed February 25, 2016. http://daniellazare.com/2014/11/12/timothy-snyder-does-it-again/.

————. "Timothy Snyder's Lies." *Jacobin*, September 9, 2014. Accessed February 25, 2016. https://www.jacobinmag.com/2014/09/timothy-snyders-lies/.

Levene, Mark. *Genocide in the Age of the Nation-State*, 2 vols. London: Routledge, 2005.

Levine, Allan. "Review: *Black Earth*, Timothy Snyder's New Book on the Origins of the Holocaust, Is Sure to Spark Controversy." *The Globe and Mail*, September 11, 2015. Accessed February 25, 2016. http://www.theglobeandmail.com/arts/books-and-media/review-black-earth-timothy-snyders-new-book-on-the-origins-of-the-holocaust-is-sure-to-spark-controversy/article26333226/.

Loeffler, James. "'In Memory of our Murdered (Jewish) Children': Hearing the Holocaust in Soviet Jewish Culture." *Slavic Review* 73, no. 3 (2014): 585–611.

Longerich, Peter. *Holocaust: The Nazi Persecution and Murder of the Jews.* Oxford: Oxford University Press, 2010.

———. *Politik der Vernichtung: Eine Gesamtdarstellung der nationalsozialistischen Judenverfolgung.* Munich: Piper, 1998.

———. *The Unwritten Order: Hitler's Role in the Final Solution.* Stroud: Tempus, 2001.

Lozny, Ludomir R. "Review of Nationalism, Marxism and Modern Central Europe: A Biography of Kazimierz Kelles-Krauz (1872–1905) by Timothy Snyder." *Canadian Slavonic Papers / Revue Canadienne des Slavistes* 42, no. 3 (2000): 369–71.

Maier, Charles S. *The Unmasterable Past: History, Holocaust, and German National Identity.* Cambridge, MA: Harvard University Press, 1988.

Mazower, Mark. *Dark Continent: Europe's Twentieth Century.* London: Penguin, 1999.

———. *Hitler's Empire: Nazi Rule in Occupied Europe.* London: Penguin, 2008.

———. "Timothy Snyder's *Bloodlands*." *Contemporary European History* 21, no. 2: 117–23.

McCauley, Justin. "Book Review: Timothy Snyder's *Bloodlands*." *The Vienna Review*, May 20, 2012. Accessed February 25, 2016. http://www.viennareview.net/vienna-review-book-reviews/book-reviews/it-tolls-for-thee.

Melson, Robert. *Revolution and Genocide: The Origins of the Armenian Genocide and the Holocaust.* Chicago: University of Chicago Press, 1992.

Mikics, David. "The Diplomat of Shoah History: Does Yale Historian Timothy Snyder Absolve Eastern Europe of Special Complicity in the Holocaust?" *Tablet*, July 26, 2012. Accessed February 25, 2016. http://www.tabletmag.com/jewish-arts-and-culture/books/107382/diplomat-of-shoah-history.

Motyl, Alexander J. "Deleting the Holodomor: Ukraine Unmakes Itself." *World Affairs* 173, no. 3 (2010), 25–34.

Moyn, Samuel. "Between Hitler and Stalin." *The Nation*, November 17, 2010. Accessed February 25, 2016. http://www.thenation.com/article/between-hitler-and-stalin/.

Muller, Adam. "Review of *Bloodlands: Europe between Hitler and Stalin* by Timothy Snyder." *The Winnipeg Review,* April 24, 2011. Accessed February 25, 2016. http://winnipegreview.com/2011/04/bloodlands-by-timothy-snyder/.

Naimark, Norman. *Stalin's Genocides.* Princeton: Princeton University Press, 2010.

Neitzel, Sönke. "Im Kerngebiet des Todes." *Frankfurter Allgemeine Zeitung*, January 29, 2012.

Nolte, Ernst. "Vergangenheit, die nicht vergehen will: Eine Rede, die geschrieben, aber nicht mehr gehalten werden konnte." *Frankfurter Allgemeine Zeitung*, June 6, 1986.

Overy, Richard. *The Dictators: Hitler's Germany, Stalin's Russia.* New York: Norton, 2004.

Penter, Tanja, *Kohle für Stalin und Hitler: Arbeiten und Leben im Donbass, 1929 bis 1953*. Essen, Klartext Verlag, 2010.

Pinto-Duschinsky, Michael. "Hitler's 'Ecological Panic' Didn't Cause the Holocaust." *Standpoint*, September 2015. Accessed February 25, 2016. http://www.standpointmag.co.uk/node/6189/full.

Pohl, Dieter. "Review of *Black Earth: The Holocaust as History and Warning* by Timothy Snyder," *H-Soz-Kult*, 15 October 2015. Accessed February 25, 2016. http://www.hsozkult.de/publicationreview/id/rezbuecher-24652.

———. *Verfolgung und Massenmord in der NS-Zeit 1933–1945*. Darmstadt: Wissenschaftliche Buchgesellschaft, 2003.

Portnov, Andriy. "On the Importance of Synthesis and the Productiveness of Comparison." In "Review Forum: Timothy Snyder, Bloodlands: Europe between Hitler and Stalin," by John Connelly, Mark Roseman, Andriy Portnov, Michael David-Fox, and Timothy Snyder, *Journal of Genocide Research* 13, no. 3 (2011): 313–52.

Prusin, Alexander V. *The Lands Between: Conflict in the East European Borderlands, 1870–1992.* Oxford: Oxford University Press, 2010.

Radio Free Europe. "Historian Timothy Snyder: 'History is Always Plural.'" *Radio Free Europe / Radio Liberty*, June 20, 2015. Accessed February 25, 2016. http://www.rferl.org/content/russia-ukraine-interview-bloodlands-timothy-snyder-history/27082683.html.

Rosenbaum, Ron. "Stalin's Cannibals. What the New Book *Bloodlands* Tells Us About the Nature of Evil." *Slate*, February 7, 2011. Accessed February

25, 2016. http://www.slate.com/articles/life/the_spectator/2011/02/stalins_
cannibals.single.html.

Roshwald, Aviel. *Ethnic Nationalism and the Fall of Empires: Central Europe, Russia and the Middle East, 1914–1923*. London: Routledge, 2001.

Rossolinski-Liebe, Grzegorz. "Debating, Obfuscating and Disciplining the Holocaust: Post-Soviet Historical Discourses on the OUN-UPA and Other Nationalist Movements." *East European Jewish Affairs* 42, no. 3 (2012): 199–241.

— — —. "Review of *Bloodlands: Europa zwischen Hitler and Stalin* by Timothy Snyder." *H-Soz-Kult*, March 30, 2011. Accessed February 25, 2016. http://www. hsozkult.de/publicationreview/id/rezbuecher-15680.

Rozett, Robert. "Diminishing the Holocaust: Scholarly Fodder for a Discourse of Distortion." *Israel Journal of Foreign Affairs* 6, no. 1 (2012): 53–64.

Sémelin, Jacques. "Snyder and His Critics." *books & ideas.net*, February 14 2013. Accessed February 25, 2016. http://www.booksandideas.net/Timothy-Snyder-and-his-Critics.html.

Simms, Brendan. "*The Red Prince* by Timothy Snyder: How the Dandy Turned Hero as Europe Burned." *The Independent*, July 11, 2008. Accessed February 25, 2016. http://www.independent.co.uk/arts-entertainment/books/reviews/the-red-prince-by-timothy-snyder-864388.html.

Snyder, Timothy. "The Battle in Ukraine Means Everything: Fascism Returns to the Continent It Once Destroyed." *New Republic*, May 11, 2014. Accessed February 25, 2016. https://newrepublic.com/article/117692/fascism-returns-ukraine.

— — —. "Beneath the Hypocrisy, Putin is Vulnerable. Here's Where His Soft Spots Are." *New Republic*, March 2, 2014. Accessed February 25, 2016. https://newrepublic.com/article/116812/how-europe-should-respond-russian-intervention-ukraine.

— — —. *Black Earth: The Holocaust as History and Warning*. London: Bodley Head, 2015.

— — —. *Bloodlands: Europe between Hitler and Stalin*. London: Vintage, 2015 (1st ed. 2010).

— — —. "The Causes of the Holocaust." *Contemporary European History* 21, no. 2 (2012): 149–68.

— — —. "The Causes of Ukrainian-Polish Ethnic Cleansing 1943." *Past and Present* 179 (2003): 197–234.

— — —. "Collaboration in the Bloodlands." *Journal of Genocide Research* 13, no. 3 (2011): 313–52.

— — —. "Edge of Europe, End of Europe." *New York Review of Books*, July 21, 2015. Accessed February 25, 2016. http://www.nybooks.com/blogs/nyrblog/2015/jul/21/ukraine-kharkiv-edge-of-europe/.

— — —. "Far-Right Forces are Influencing Russia's Actions in Crimea." *New Republic*, March 17, 2014. Accessed February 25, 2016. https://newrepublic.com/article/117048/far-right-forces-are-influencing-russias-actions-crimea.

— — —. "A Fascist Hero in Democratic Kiev." *New York Review of Books*, February 24, 2010.

— — —. "Holocaust: The Ignored Reality." *New York Review of Books*, July 16, 2009. Accessed February 25, 2016. http://www.nybooks.com/articles/archives/2009/jul/16/holocaust-the-ignored-reality/.

— — —. "In Defense of *Bloodlands*." *Tablet*, August 3, 2012. Accessed February 25, 2016. http://www.tabletmag.com/jewish-arts-and-culture/books/108229/in-defense-of-bloodlands.

— — —. "The Life and Death of Western Volhynian Jewry, 1921–1945." In Ray Brandon and Wendy Lower, eds, *The Shoah in Ukraine: History, Testimony, Memorialization,* 77–113. Bloomington: Indiana University Press, 2008.

— — —. "Memory of Sovereignty and Sovereignty over Memory: Poland, Lithuania and Ukraine, 1939–1999." In Jan-Werner Müller (ed.), *Memory and Power in Post-war Europe*, 39–58. Cambridge: Cambridge University Press, 2004.

— — —. *Nationalism, Marxism, and Modern Central Europe: A Biography of Kazimierz Kelles-Krauz (1872–1905)*. Cambridge, MA: Harvard University Press, 1998.

— — —. "Nazis, Soviets, Poles, Jews." *New York Review of Books*, December 3, 2009. Accessed February 25, 2016. http://www.nybooks.com/articles/archives/2009/dec/03/nazis-soviets-poles-jews/#fnr1-316546747.

— — —. "A New Approach to the Holocaust." *New York Review of Books*, June 23, 2011. Accessed February 25, 2016. http://www.nybooks.com/articles/archives/2011/jun/23/new-approach-holocaust/#fn-7.

— — —. "Putin's New Nostalgia." *New York Review of Books*, November 10, 2014. Accessed February 25, 2016. http://www.nybooks.com/blogs/nyrblog/2014/nov/10/putin-nostalgia-stalin-hitler/.

— — —. *The Reconstruction of Nations: Poland, Ukraine, Lithuania, Belarus, 1569–1999*. New Haven: Yale University Press, 2003.

— — —. *The Red Prince: The Fall of a Dynasty and the Rise of Modern Europe*. London: Bodley Head, 2008.

———. "To Resolve the Ukrainian Problem Once and for All: The Ethnic Cleansing of Ukrainians in Poland, 1943–1947." *Journal of Cold War Studies* 1, no. 2 (1999): 86–120.

———. *Sketches from a Secret War: A Polish Artist's Mission to Liberate Soviet Ukraine*. New Haven: Yale University Press, 2005.

———. "Ukrainian Extremists Will Only Triumph if Russia Invades." *New Republic*, April 17, 2014. Accessed February 25, 2016. https://newrepublic. com/article/117395/historic-ukrainian-russian-relations-impact-maidan-revolution.

Snyder, Timothy, and Timothy Garton Ash. "The Orange Revolution." *New York Review of Books*, April 28, 2005. Accessed February 25, 2016. http://www. nybooks.com/articles/archives/2005/apr/28/the-orange-revolution/.

Spaulding, Norman W. "Resistance, Countermemory, Justice." *Critical Enquiry* 41, no. 1 (2014): 132–52.

Streit, Christian. *Keine Kameraden: Die Wehrmacht und die sowjetischen Kriegsgefangenen 1941–1945*. Bonn: Dietz, 1991.

Thomson, Ian. "Review of *Bloodlands: Europe between Hitler and Stalin* by Timothy Snyder." *The Telegraph*, November 9, 2010. Accessed February 25, 2016. http://www.telegraph.co.uk/culture/books/bookreviews/8120244/ Bloodlands-Europe-Between-Hitler-and-Stalin-review.html.

Times Higher Education editors. "Review of Bloodlands: Europe between Hitler and Stalin by Timothy Snyder." *Times Higher Education*, January 27, 2011. Accessed February 25, 2016. https://www.timeshighereducation.com/books/ bloodlands-europe-between-hitler-and-stalin/414946.article.

Truchlewski, Zbigniew. "Timothy Snyder, A Historian of Eastern Europe." *Nouvelle Europe*, February 11, 2013. Accessed February 25, 2016. http://www. nouvelle-europe.eu/node/1640.

Viola, Lynne. *Peasant Rebels Under Stalin: Collectivization and the Culture of Peasant Resistance*. New York: Oxford University Press, 1996.

———. *The Unknown Gulag: The Lost World of Stalin's Special Settlements*. New York: Oxford University Press, 2007.

von Hagen, Mark. "Empires, Borderlands and Diasporas: Eurasia as Anti-Paradigm for the Post-Soviet Era." *American Historical Review* 109, no. 2 (2004): 445–68.

Werth, Nicholas. *La terreur et le désarroi: Staline et son système*. Paris: Perrin, 2007.

Wildt, Michael. *An Uncompromising Generation: The Nazi Leadership of the Reich Security Main Office*. Madison: University of Wisconsin Press, 2010.

————. "Review of *Bloodlands: Europe between Hitler and Stalin* by Timothy Snyder." *Kritika: Explorations in Russian and Eurasian History* 14, no. 1 (2013): 197–206.

Yale University Department of History. "Timothy Snyder." Yale University Department of History website. Accessed February 25, 2016. http://history.yale.edu/people/timothy-snyder.

Yale University Press. *The Reconstruction of Nations: Poland, Ukraine, Lithuania, Belarus*, 1569–1999 by Timothy Snyder. Yale University Press website. Accessed March 1, 2016. http://history.yale.edu/timothy-snyder/reconstruction-nations-poland-ukraine-lithuana-belarus-1569-1999.

Yerxa, Donald A. "*Bloodlands: Europe between Hitler and Stalin*: An Interview with Timothy Snyder." *Historically Speaking* 12, no. 5 (2011): 29–30.

Zahra, Tara. "Imagined Noncommunities: National Indifference as a Category of Analysis." *Slavic Review* 69, no. 1 (2010): 93–119.

Zarusky, Jürgen. "Timothy Snyder's 'Bloodlands': Kritische Anmerkungen zur Konstruktion einer Geschichtslandschaft." *Vierteljahrshefte für Zeitgeschichte* 60, no. 1 (2012): 1–31.

THE MACAT LIBRARY
BY DISCIPLINE

AFRICANA STUDIES

Chinua Achebe's *An Image of Africa: Racism in Conrad's Heart of Darkness*
W. E. B. Du Bois's *The Souls of Black Folk*
Zora Neale Huston's *Characteristics of Negro Expression*
Martin Luther King Jr's *Why We Can't Wait*
Toni Morrison's *Playing in the Dark: Whiteness in the American Literary Imagination*

ANTHROPOLOGY

Arjun Appadurai's *Modernity at Large: Cultural Dimensions of Globalisation*
Philippe Ariès's *Centuries of Childhood*
Franz Boas's *Race, Language and Culture*
Kim Chan & Renée Mauborgne's *Blue Ocean Strategy*
Jared Diamond's *Guns, Germs & Steel: the Fate of Human Societies*
Jared Diamond's *Collapse: How Societies Choose to Fail or Survive*
E. E. Evans-Pritchard's *Witchcraft, Oracles and Magic Among the Azande*
James Ferguson's *The Anti-Politics Machine*
Clifford Geertz's *The Interpretation of Cultures*
David Graeber's *Debt: the First 5000 Years*
Karen Ho's *Liquidated: An Ethnography of Wall Street*
Geert Hofstede's *Culture's Consequences: Comparing Values, Behaviors, Institutes and Organizations across Nations*
Claude Lévi-Strauss's *Structural Anthropology*
Jay Macleod's *Ain't No Makin' It: Aspirations and Attainment in a Low-Income Neighborhood*
Saba Mahmood's *The Politics of Piety: The Islamic Revival and the Feminist Subject*
Marcel Mauss's *The Gift*

BUSINESS

Jean Lave & Etienne Wenger's *Situated Learning*
Theodore Levitt's *Marketing Myopia*
Burton G. Malkiel's *A Random Walk Down Wall Street*
Douglas McGregor's *The Human Side of Enterprise*
Michael Porter's *Competitive Strategy: Creating and Sustaining Superior Performance*
John Kotter's *Leading Change*
C. K. Prahalad & Gary Hamel's *The Core Competence of the Corporation*

CRIMINOLOGY

Michelle Alexander's *The New Jim Crow: Mass Incarceration in the Age of Colorblindness*
Michael R. Gottfredson & Travis Hirschi's *A General Theory of Crime*
Richard Herrnstein & Charles A. Murray's *The Bell Curve: Intelligence and Class Structure in American Life*
Elizabeth Loftus's *Eyewitness Testimony*
Jay Macleod's *Ain't No Makin' It: Aspirations and Attainment in a Low-Income Neighborhood*
Philip Zimbardo's *The Lucifer Effect*

ECONOMICS

Janet Abu-Lughod's *Before European Hegemony*
Ha-Joon Chang's *Kicking Away the Ladder*
David Brion Davis's *The Problem of Slavery in the Age of Revolution*
Milton Friedman's *The Role of Monetary Policy*
Milton Friedman's *Capitalism and Freedom*
David Graeber's *Debt: the First 5000 Years*
Friedrich Hayek's *The Road to Serfdom*
Karen Ho's *Liquidated: An Ethnography of Wall Street*

John Maynard Keynes's *The General Theory of Employment, Interest and Money*
Charles P. Kindleberger's *Manias, Panics and Crashes*
Robert Lucas's *Why Doesn't Capital Flow from Rich to Poor Countries?*
Burton G. Malkiel's *A Random Walk Down Wall Street*
Thomas Robert Malthus's *An Essay on the Principle of Population*
Karl Marx's *Capital*
Thomas Piketty's *Capital in the Twenty-First Century*
Amartya Sen's *Development as Freedom*
Adam Smith's *The Wealth of Nations*
Nassim Nicholas Taleb's *The Black Swan: The Impact of the Highly Improbable*
Amos Tversky's & Daniel Kahneman's *Judgment under Uncertainty: Heuristics and Biases*
Mahbub Ul Haq's *Reflections on Human Development*
Max Weber's *The Protestant Ethic and the Spirit of Capitalism*

FEMINISM AND GENDER STUDIES

Judith Butler's *Gender Trouble*
Simone De Beauvoir's *The Second Sex*
Michel Foucault's *History of Sexuality*
Betty Friedan's *The Feminine Mystique*
Saba Mahmood's *The Politics of Piety: The Islamic Revival and the Feminist Subject*
Joan Wallach Scott's *Gender and the Politics of History*
Mary Wollstonecraft's *A Vindication of the Rights of Woman*
Virginia Woolf's *A Room of One's Own*

GEOGRAPHY

The Brundtland Report's *Our Common Future*
Rachel Carson's *Silent Spring*
Charles Darwin's *On the Origin of Species*
James Ferguson's *The Anti-Politics Machine*
Jane Jacobs's *The Death and Life of Great American Cities*
James Lovelock's *Gaia: A New Look at Life on Earth*
Amartya Sen's *Development as Freedom*
Mathis Wackernagel & William Rees's *Our Ecological Footprint*

HISTORY

Janet Abu-Lughod's *Before European Hegemony*
Benedict Anderson's *Imagined Communities*
Bernard Bailyn's *The Ideological Origins of the American Revolution*
Hanna Batatu's *The Old Social Classes And The Revolutionary Movements Of Iraq*
Christopher Browning's *Ordinary Men: Reserve Police Batallion 101 and the Final Solution in Poland*
Edmund Burke's *Reflections on the Revolution in France*
William Cronon's *Nature's Metropolis: Chicago And The Great West*
Alfred W. Crosby's *The Columbian Exchange*
Hamid Dabashi's *Iran: A People Interrupted*
David Brion Davis's *The Problem of Slavery in the Age of Revolution*
Nathalie Zemon Davis's *The Return of Martin Guerre*
Jared Diamond's *Guns, Germs & Steel: the Fate of Human Societies*
Frank Dikotter's *Mao's Great Famine*
John W Dower's *War Without Mercy: Race And Power In The Pacific War*
W. E. B. Du Bois's *The Souls of Black Folk*
Richard J. Evans's *In Defence of History*
Lucien Febvre's *The Problem of Unbelief in the 16th Century*
Sheila Fitzpatrick's *Everyday Stalinism*

Eric Foner's *Reconstruction: America's Unfinished Revolution, 1863-1877*
Michel Foucault's *Discipline and Punish*
Michel Foucault's *History of Sexuality*
Francis Fukuyama's *The End of History and the Last Man*
John Lewis Gaddis's *We Now Know: Rethinking Cold War History*
Ernest Gellner's *Nations and Nationalism*
Eugene Genovese's *Roll, Jordan, Roll: The World the Slaves Made*
Carlo Ginzburg's *The Night Battles*
Daniel Goldhagen's *Hitler's Willing Executioners*
Jack Goldstone's *Revolution and Rebellion in the Early Modern World*
Antonio Gramsci's *The Prison Notebooks*
Alexander Hamilton, John Jay & James Madison's *The Federalist Papers*
Christopher Hill's *The World Turned Upside Down*
Carole Hillenbrand's *The Crusades: Islamic Perspectives*
Thomas Hobbes's *Leviathan*
Eric Hobsbawm's *The Age Of Revolution*
John A. Hobson's *Imperialism: A Study*
Albert Hourani's *History of the Arab Peoples*
Samuel P. Huntington's *The Clash of Civilizations and the Remaking of World Order*
C. L. R. James's *The Black Jacobins*
Tony Judt's *Postwar: A History of Europe Since 1945*
Ernst Kantorowicz's *The King's Two Bodies: A Study in Medieval Political Theology*
Paul Kennedy's *The Rise and Fall of the Great Powers*
Ian Kershaw's *The "Hitler Myth": Image and Reality in the Third Reich*
John Maynard Keynes's *The General Theory of Employment, Interest and Money*
Charles P. Kindleberger's *Manias, Panics and Crashes*
Martin Luther King Jr's *Why We Can't Wait*
Henry Kissinger's *World Order: Reflections on the Character of Nations and the Course of History*
Thomas Kuhn's *The Structure of Scientific Revolutions*
Georges Lefebvre's *The Coming of the French Revolution*
John Locke's *Two Treatises of Government*
Niccolò Machiavelli's *The Prince*
Thomas Robert Malthus's *An Essay on the Principle of Population*
Mahmood Mamdani's *Citizen and Subject: Contemporary Africa And The Legacy Of Late Colonialism*
Karl Marx's *Capital*
Stanley Milgram's *Obedience to Authority*
John Stuart Mill's *On Liberty*
Thomas Paine's *Common Sense*
Thomas Paine's *Rights of Man*
Geoffrey Parker's *Global Crisis: War, Climate Change and Catastrophe in the Seventeenth Century*
Jonathan Riley-Smith's *The First Crusade and the Idea of Crusading*
Jean-Jacques Rousseau's *The Social Contract*
Joan Wallach Scott's *Gender and the Politics of History*
Theda Skocpol's *States and Social Revolutions*
Adam Smith's *The Wealth of Nations*
Timothy Snyder's *Bloodlands: Europe Between Hitler and Stalin*
Sun Tzu's *The Art of War*
Keith Thomas's *Religion and the Decline of Magic*
Thucydides's *The History of the Peloponnesian War*
Frederick Jackson Turner's *The Significance of the Frontier in American History*
Odd Arne Westad's *The Global Cold War: Third World Interventions And The Making Of Our Times*

LITERATURE

Chinua Achebe's *An Image of Africa: Racism in Conrad's Heart of Darkness*
Roland Barthes's *Mythologies*
Homi K. Bhabha's *The Location of Culture*
Judith Butler's *Gender Trouble*
Simone De Beauvoir's *The Second Sex*
Ferdinand De Saussure's *Course in General Linguistics*
T. S. Eliot's *The Sacred Wood: Essays on Poetry and Criticism*
Zora Neale Huston's *Characteristics of Negro Expression*
Toni Morrison's *Playing in the Dark: Whiteness in the American Literary Imagination*
Edward Said's *Orientalism*
Gayatri Chakravorty Spivak's *Can the Subaltern Speak?*
Mary Wollstonecraft's *A Vindication of the Rights of Women*
Virginia Woolf's *A Room of One's Own*

PHILOSOPHY

Elizabeth Anscombe's *Modern Moral Philosophy*
Hannah Arendt's *The Human Condition*
Aristotle's *Metaphysics*
Aristotle's *Nicomachean Ethics*
Edmund Gettier's *Is Justified True Belief Knowledge?*
Georg Wilhelm Friedrich Hegel's *Phenomenology of Spirit*
David Hume's *Dialogues Concerning Natural Religion*
David Hume's *The Enquiry for Human Understanding*
Immanuel Kant's *Religion within the Boundaries of Mere Reason*
Immanuel Kant's *Critique of Pure Reason*
Søren Kierkegaard's *The Sickness Unto Death*
Søren Kierkegaard's *Fear and Trembling*
C. S. Lewis's *The Abolition of Man*
Alasdair MacIntyre's *After Virtue*
Marcus Aurelius's *Meditations*
Friedrich Nietzsche's *On the Genealogy of Morality*
Friedrich Nietzsche's *Beyond Good and Evil*
Plato's *Republic*
Plato's *Symposium*
Jean-Jacques Rousseau's *The Social Contract*
Gilbert Ryle's *The Concept of Mind*
Baruch Spinoza's *Ethics*
Sun Tzu's *The Art of War*
Ludwig Wittgenstein's *Philosophical Investigations*

POLITICS

Benedict Anderson's *Imagined Communities*
Aristotle's *Politics*
Bernard Bailyn's *The Ideological Origins of the American Revolution*
Edmund Burke's *Reflections on the Revolution in France*
John C. Calhoun's *A Disquisition on Government*
Ha-Joon Chang's *Kicking Away the Ladder*
Hamid Dabashi's *Iran: A People Interrupted*
Hamid Dabashi's *Theology of Discontent: The Ideological Foundation of the Islamic Revolution in Iran*
Robert Dahl's *Democracy and its Critics*
Robert Dahl's *Who Governs?*
David Brion Davis's *The Problem of Slavery in the Age of Revolution*

Alexis De Tocqueville's *Democracy in America*
James Ferguson's *The Anti-Politics Machine*
Frank Dikotter's *Mao's Great Famine*
Sheila Fitzpatrick's *Everyday Stalinism*
Eric Foner's *Reconstruction: America's Unfinished Revolution, 1863-1877*
Milton Friedman's *Capitalism and Freedom*
Francis Fukuyama's *The End of History and the Last Man*
John Lewis Gaddis's *We Now Know: Rethinking Cold War History*
Ernest Gellner's *Nations and Nationalism*
David Graeber's *Debt: the First 5000 Years*
Antonio Gramsci's *The Prison Notebooks*
Alexander Hamilton, John Jay & James Madison's *The Federalist Papers*
Friedrich Hayek's *The Road to Serfdom*
Christopher Hill's *The World Turned Upside Down*
Thomas Hobbes's *Leviathan*
John A. Hobson's *Imperialism: A Study*
Samuel P. Huntington's *The Clash of Civilizations and the Remaking of World Order*
Tony Judt's *Postwar: A History of Europe Since 1945*
David C. Kang's *China Rising: Peace, Power and Order in East Asia*
Paul Kennedy's *The Rise and Fall of Great Powers*
Robert Keohane's *After Hegemony*
Martin Luther King Jr.'s *Why We Can't Wait*
Henry Kissinger's *World Order: Reflections on the Character of Nations and the Course of History*
John Locke's *Two Treatises of Government*
Niccolò Machiavelli's *The Prince*
Thomas Robert Malthus's *An Essay on the Principle of Population*
Mahmood Mamdani's *Citizen and Subject: Contemporary Africa And The Legacy Of Late Colonialism*
Karl Marx's *Capital*
John Stuart Mill's *On Liberty*
John Stuart Mill's *Utilitarianism*
Hans Morgenthau's *Politics Among Nations*
Thomas Paine's *Common Sense*
Thomas Paine's *Rights of Man*
Thomas Piketty's *Capital in the Twenty-First Century*
Robert D. Putman's *Bowling Alone*
John Rawls's *Theory of Justice*
Jean-Jacques Rousseau's *The Social Contract*
Theda Skocpol's *States and Social Revolutions*
Adam Smith's *The Wealth of Nations*
Sun Tzu's *The Art of War*
Henry David Thoreau's *Civil Disobedience*
Thucydides's *The History of the Peloponnesian War*
Kenneth Waltz's *Theory of International Politics*
Max Weber's *Politics as a Vocation*
Odd Arne Westad's *The Global Cold War: Third World Interventions And The Making Of Our Times*

POSTCOLONIAL STUDIES

Roland Barthes's *Mythologies*
Frantz Fanon's *Black Skin, White Masks*
Homi K. Bhabha's *The Location of Culture*
Gustavo Gutiérrez's *A Theology of Liberation*
Edward Said's *Orientalism*
Gayatri Chakravorty Spivak's *Can the Subaltern Speak?*

PSYCHOLOGY

Gordon Allport's *The Nature of Prejudice*
Alan Baddeley & Graham Hitch's *Aggression: A Social Learning Analysis*
Albert Bandura's *Aggression: A Social Learning Analysis*
Leon Festinger's *A Theory of Cognitive Dissonance*
Sigmund Freud's *The Interpretation of Dreams*
Betty Friedan's *The Feminine Mystique*
Michael R. Gottfredson & Travis Hirschi's *A General Theory of Crime*
Eric Hoffer's *The True Believer: Thoughts on the Nature of Mass Movements*
William James's *Principles of Psychology*
Elizabeth Loftus's *Eyewitness Testimony*
A. H. Maslow's *A Theory of Human Motivation*
Stanley Milgram's *Obedience to Authority*
Steven Pinker's *The Better Angels of Our Nature*
Oliver Sacks's *The Man Who Mistook His Wife For a Hat*
Richard Thaler & Cass Sunstein's *Nudge: Improving Decisions About Health, Wealth and Happiness*
Amos Tversky's *Judgment under Uncertainty: Heuristics and Biases*
Philip Zimbardo's *The Lucifer Effect*

SCIENCE

Rachel Carson's *Silent Spring*
William Cronon's *Nature's Metropolis: Chicago And The Great West*
Alfred W. Crosby's *The Columbian Exchange*
Charles Darwin's *On the Origin of Species*
Richard Dawkin's *The Selfish Gene*
Thomas Kuhn's *The Structure of Scientific Revolutions*
Geoffrey Parker's *Global Crisis: War, Climate Change and Catastrophe in the Seventeenth Century*
Mathis Wackernagel & William Rees's *Our Ecological Footprint*

SOCIOLOGY

Michelle Alexander's *The New Jim Crow: Mass Incarceration in the Age of Colorblindness*
Gordon Allport's *The Nature of Prejudice*
Albert Bandura's *Aggression: A Social Learning Analysis*
Hanna Batatu's *The Old Social Classes And The Revolutionary Movements Of Iraq*
Ha-Joon Chang's *Kicking Away the Ladder*
W. E. B. Du Bois's *The Souls of Black Folk*
Émile Durkheim's *On Suicide*
Frantz Fanon's *Black Skin, White Masks*
Frantz Fanon's *The Wretched of the Earth*
Eric Foner's *Reconstruction: America's Unfinished Revolution, 1863-1877*
Eugene Genovese's *Roll, Jordan, Roll: The World the Slaves Made*
Jack Goldstone's *Revolution and Rebellion in the Early Modern World*
Antonio Gramsci's *The Prison Notebooks*
Richard Herrnstein & Charles A Murray's *The Bell Curve: Intelligence and Class Structure in American Life*
Eric Hoffer's *The True Believer: Thoughts on the Nature of Mass Movements*
Jane Jacobs's *The Death and Life of Great American Cities*
Robert Lucas's *Why Doesn't Capital Flow from Rich to Poor Countries?*
Jay Macleod's *Ain't No Makin' It: Aspirations and Attainment in a Low Income Neighborhood*
Elaine May's *Homeward Bound: American Families in the Cold War Era*
Douglas McGregor's *The Human Side of Enterprise*
C. Wright Mills's *The Sociological Imagination*

Thomas Piketty's *Capital in the Twenty-First Century*
Robert D. Putman's *Bowling Alone*
David Riesman's *The Lonely Crowd: A Study of the Changing American Character*
Edward Said's *Orientalism*
Joan Wallach Scott's *Gender and the Politics of History*
Theda Skocpol's *States and Social Revolutions*
Max Weber's *The Protestant Ethic and the Spirit of Capitalism*

THEOLOGY

Augustine's *Confessions*
Benedict's *Rule of St Benedict*
Gustavo Gutiérrez's *A Theology of Liberation*
Carole Hillenbrand's *The Crusades: Islamic Perspectives*
David Hume's *Dialogues Concerning Natural Religion*
Immanuel Kant's *Religion within the Boundaries of Mere Reason*
Ernst Kantorowicz's *The King's Two Bodies: A Study in Medieval Political Theology*
Søren Kierkegaard's *The Sickness Unto Death*
C. S. Lewis's *The Abolition of Man*
Saba Mahmood's *The Politics of Piety: The Islamic Revival and the Feminist Subject*
Baruch Spinoza's *Ethics*
Keith Thomas's *Religion and the Decline of Magic*

COMING SOON

Chris Argyris's *The Individual and the Organisation*
Seyla Benhabib's *The Rights of Others*
Walter Benjamin's *The Work Of Art in the Age of Mechanical Reproduction*
John Berger's *Ways of Seeing*
Pierre Bourdieu's *Outline of a Theory of Practice*
Mary Douglas's *Purity and Danger*
Roland Dworkin's *Taking Rights Seriously*
James G. March's *Exploration and Exploitation in Organisational Learning*
Ikujiro Nonaka's *A Dynamic Theory of Organizational Knowledge Creation*
Griselda Pollock's *Vision and Difference*
Amartya Sen's *Inequality Re-Examined*
Susan Sontag's *On Photography*
Yasser Tabbaa's *The Transformation of Islamic Art*
Ludwig von Mises's *Theory of Money and Credit*

Macat Disciplines

Access the greatest ideas and thinkers across entire disciplines, including

AFRICANA STUDIES

Chinua Achebe's *An Image of Africa: Racism in Conrad's Heart of Darkness*

W. E. B. Du Bois's *The Souls of Black Folk*

Zora Neale Hurston's *Characteristics of Negro Expression*

Martin Luther King Jr.'s *Why We Can't Wait*

Toni Morrison's *Playing in the Dark: Whiteness in the American Literary Imagination*